Family Restructuring Therapy

Interventions
with
High Conflict
Separations
and Divorces

Stephen Carter, Ph.D.

HCI Press
Scottsdale, Arizona

A Note to the Reader

This publication is designed to provide accurate and authoritative information in regard to the subject matter concerned. It is sold with the understanding that the publisher and author are not engaged in rendering psychological, legal, financial, or other professional advice to the general public.

Names in the book are completely fictional.

Laws are constantly changing and are different in each state, province and country. You should not rely in any way on this book for specific legal information or therapeutic advice. The purpose is to educate the reader about a process used by the author in his work to handle cases of this type. The publisher and author are not responsible for personal decisions or interpretations of the information provided herein.

Copyright © 2011 by Steven Carter
     HCI Press
     7701 E. Indian School Rd. Ste. F
     Scottsdale, AZ 85251
     www.hcipress.com

Library of Congress Control Number: 2011930464

ISBN-13: 978-1-936268-39-9
ISBN-10: 1-936268-39-6

Book Design by Karrie Ross, www.KarrieRoss.com

High Conflict Institute Press
Scottsdale, Arizona

Acknowledgements

My number one thank you goes to my wife Lori who has edited everything I have ever written to do with psychology. Also immensely important are my practice partners, Dr. Bonnie Haave, Dr. Shirley Vandersteen, and Mr. Jim Bateman, our associates at Carter Haave Vandersteen Bateman and our office manager, Patty, who are all part of the team in working with high-conflict families. This book represents the collective knowledge of all of us and has evolved over almost 20 years of working together.

A special thank you goes out to retired Court of Queen's Bench Justice, the Honourable Marguerite Trussler; to the families we have worked with who "got it" and made life better for their children; and for the children involved, who are often our best teachers.

Introduction

Family Restructuring Therapy is an active, therapist-directed process for working with divorced families ranging from the "normal" divorced family who needs to learn new practices and patterns, to the "high-conflict" family whose behaviour patterns have become so maladaptive that the children's well-being is at risk. While this book is written for the mental health practitioner it can also be a valuable resource for lawyers and the Court when trying to decide what can be done with challenging parenting situations where the parents are no longer together and are often locked in an ongoing battle.

A key focus of this book is looking at the needs of the child within the family, while never losing sight of the fact the children need their parents to make the tough decisions and to act like adults. It is clearly not a passive approach to counselling. The goal is not for parents to self-actualize or to gain insight; the goal is for the parents "to do their divorce better than they did their marriage" and to learn how to communicate, parent, and behave appropriately.

Contents

Foreword

An Australian family court judge once said to me that in family law cases, the 10% of cases that are high-conflict take up 90% of the Court's time. From my experience, he is correct. Yet the courtroom is the worst place for these cases because the adversarial system increases the conflict.

After one particularly difficult case, I came to the conclusion there had to be a better way to deal with these cases. I did not have the background or training to deal with them effectively. In addition, a judge only sees a snapshot at one particular time in the parents' lives, particularly on a preliminary motion. The affidavits that are filed in preliminary motions are always contradictory.

I turned to a firm of local psychologists for assistance. Dr. Stephen Carter was one of those psychologists. The firm developed Family Restructuring Therapy. When a matter came before me and there appeared to be unresolved conflict, I referred the file to them. It was suggested that parties could not afford the cost but it turned out to be less for 10 hours of therapy than a contested court application, and a fraction of the cost of a bilateral custody assessment. A majority of the files were resolved by this therapy. Of those that were not resolved, the report from the therapist often gave me a clear picture of the family dynamics and what should be done to best protect the children. There were some files, particularly where there where addiction issues or personality disorders, where the best that could be done was to order a bilateral custody assessment and schedule an early trial, but it was extremely helpful to have these files identified at an early stage.

It is better to refer files when the conflict is not entrenched by time and numerous court applications. However, there were times when files, with multiple applications and several case management judges over a number of years, responded to Family Restructuring Therapy. I found that working as a team with the psychologists who used Family Restructuring Therapy made decision making much easier, helped families quickly find a new working relationship and do significantly less damage to their children during the divorce process.

I am pleased that Dr. Carter has taken the time to write a book to share his successful methods to resolve family conflict.

Hon. Marguerite Trussler

Edmonton, Alberta

February 19, 2011

PART I

Background

Introduction to
Family Restructuring Therapy

Family Restructuring Therapy is the philosophy and process of working with high-conflict families of separation and divorce. It is not new. Family Restructuring Therapy got its start some 20 years ago when the Honourable Madam Justice Marguerite Trussler had a conversation with Psychologist Dr. Bonnie Haave about a high-conflict case and stated that there had to be an alternative to a custody assessment. Since then it has evolved and has been presented first as Restoring the Family System: Addressing Alienation (Carter, S., Chandler, C., Haave, B., Vandersteen, S., Trussler, M. Presentation at the Fourth International Symposium on Child Custody Evaluations, November 9-11, 2000. Association of Family and Conciliation Courts, South Carolina.). Later, as we strove to explain to others what we do, the name went from Parental Conflict Intervention to Family Restructuring Therapy in subsequent presentations in Canada and the United States.

The goal of this book is to be a written "how to" manual for working with separated and divorced families. While we started with high-conflict cases, the principles apply equally well to lower-conflict separations. It is expected that mental health professionals engaged in Family Restructuring Therapy have a background that includes training and practice providing therapy to children, couples and families; knowledge of child and family development; and the impact of family conflict and divorce on children and adults. Understanding issues pertaining to child abuse, neglect and family violence and false allegations is also important; as is knowledge of laws and procedures pertaining to custody issues for the local jurisdiction.

The definition of family comes
from the child's perspective,
whatever the original configuration
of the family.

Most important, Family Restructuring Therapy is an active, directive therapeutic process. The mental health professional in this process is more concerned with how a parent behaves than with how he or she feels. **The definition of family comes from the child's perspective, whatever the original configuration of the family.** Parents can divorce, families cannot. Throughout this book the focus is to help the family transition towards a healthy functioning unit. Neither parent can win; the only people who win or lose in a divorce are the children. Children win when they have meaningful involvement with as many behaviourally and emotionally healthy and appropriate parents as they can have.

To streamline reading, two definitions are provided:

- A "parent" can be a biological parent, an adoptive parent, a stepparent who has been in a significant parental role, a parent from a mixed-gender relationship or a parent from a same-gender relationship.
- "Divorce" will be used to refer to parents who are no longer together and can include those who were married,

those who were in a non-marital relationship and those who had a brief encounter creating a pregnancy.

I acknowledge all of the different combinations of family we have and will not waste further time and complicate the reading by referring to all possible combinations each time.

Family violence and child abuse are real and pervasive problems. They are within the context of divorced families; however, also present are false allegations in custody battles. Family Restructuring Therapy cannot be used when significant, un-investigated allegations exist and when a child protection assessment or child custody assessment would be a more suitable intervention. Family Restructuring Therapy can be used after allegations are examined and found unsubstantiated as this is a common element of high-conflict custody battles.

The parents referred to in various examples during the book (Pat Smith and Kelly Wesson, and their children Kim and Jordan) are entirely fictitious, and purposely gender-neutral names.

The Philosophy and Theory
of Family Resturcturing Therapy

Family Restructuring Therapy is an active, directive process that assists families in conflict to modify maladaptive interactions. It can also be used to assist lower-conflict "normal" families to heal from divorce and to move toward a new level of cooperation and functionality.

Family Restructuring Therapy is future-oriented and action-focused. It teaches parents to co-parent, to develop concrete and practical parenting plans, and can also work in reuniting parents with alienated children. The central focus is the needs of the children. Children need as many healthy and appropriate parents meaningfully involved in their lives as possible. Children do not need to be thrust into making adult decisions, such as how to divide up their time between parents, and they need to be protected from parental conflict. The next chapter will address these issues in more detail.

The problems that exist in high-conflict divorced families are not limited to one family member; all family members are affected. It is for this reason that a systemic approach is utilized that views the family system as the client, rather than the individual members. The family members all own part of the symptoms, so all family members must be part of the treatment. As a therapist, many times I have been asked to see a child individually from a split family that is not doing well. Typically, I refuse. What I tell the parents instead is that I first need to meet with the parents to see:

(a) if they have the same view of the child's symptoms,

(b) if there are divorce issues which are likely creating stress on the child,

(c) how they are attempting to treat the child's symptoms, and

(d) whether it is a problem that should be treated through individual counselling with the child or if, in fact, the work needs to be done first with the parents to see if they can make changes that allow the child to be healthier.

Family Restructuring Therapy makes an explicit demand for family members to change observable behaviours. It can go as far as telling the parent, "I expect you to change how you behave, not necessarily how you feel". The focus is on what takes place between family members more so than what is going on within each family member. This approach examines interactions between different subsystems as well as the system as a whole. Another aspect of the family being a system is that systems are resistant to change. It is for this reason that nondirective talk therapy at best does not work with high-conflict divorce families and at worst exacerbates the problems.

Family Restructuring Therapy "blames" the family dynamic and ineffective patterns of problem-solving and communication, rather than pointing fingers at an individual. Even in an extreme case where there has been an alienated child, the goal is not to have the child establish a relationship with the estranged parent and see that the alienating parent is evil; instead, the goal is to have the child meaningfully involved with both parents.

The goal of Family Restructuring Therapy is to effect a change in the family system...

It is easier to be successful when the therapist is able to blame the processes (communication, problem solving, rule setting, etc.) rather than blaming individual members. All family members are seen to be part of the problem and all family members are seen to be part of the solution, with the vast majority of responsibility being placed squarely upon the parents to act like parents/adults. **The goal of Family Restructuring Therapy is to effect a change in the family system which reflects the changes to the structure of the family created by the divorce.**

Family Restructuring Therapy is an educational process as well as a therapeutic one. The parents are taught to understand the effect that conflict and divorce have on children and are encouraged to view the family from the child's perspective, not from their own perspective. The parents need to be taught to communicate, perhaps better than ever before, regarding the needs of the children while also establishing firm personal boundaries to prevent their own personal relationship difficulties from negatively affecting their role as co-parents.

I have often told parents that they need to view the situation as if they are living in a "divorce duplex" in which the child has his or her own door to move back and forth, but that there is a wall the parents cannot pass through which represents their personal boundaries. In the divorce duplex you can hear what is going on over the fence and sometimes even see the other side. However, unless invited, or in the case of an extreme emergency, each parent must respect the privacy of the other parent.

Simply put, with Family Restructuring Therapy, the therapist is a teacher, coach, parenting expert and advisor who utilizes his or her extensive experience working with families to lead the families into a new, productive level of functioning. The therapist takes control of the parenting relationship, addresses practical aspects of communication, problem solving and parenting, while leaving the responsibility for parenting to the parents.

The importance of being future-oriented cannot be overstated. I have an initial individual session with each parent where I often state, "This session allows you to tell me the whole story just so you know that I have heard it. It is not really important that I do hear it, but after today I am not going to let you talk about the past; as the only part of your lives we can influence is the present and the future." Talking about past issues tends to have a focus on laying blame, and, as all memory is imperfect and biased, and given the fact that mental health professionals cannot read minds, the absolute truth about previous events can never be known. So rather than discussing whose fault it was that an important school project was not exchanged at the last transfer of the children, the discussion focuses on how transfers in the future can be more effective.

Developmental Advantages and Disadvantages of Shared Parenting

Definitions

"Shared parenting" is not a new concept. It was referred to by Taylor in 1989 as a new way for parents to describe their desire to remain actively involved with their children, despite the demise of the nuclear family structure. Taylor further pointed out that some intact families would not meet the definition for shared parenting and that it is largely determined by time availability, parental skill and desire.

Many terms, and even more definitions, exist regarding parental involvement with their children after divorce. Terms such as custody, access, residence and parenting are combined with other terms such as sole, joint, dual and primary. Often, financial obligations and time limits accompany such definitions. For example, in Canada, shared custody is defined as an arrangement in which the children spend a minimum of 40% of the time living with each parent, an arrangement that has significant implications on child support payments. American definitions separate *legal shared parenting*, where decision-making is shared, and *physical shared parenting*, where the children move residences each week (Benjamin & Irving, 1989).

For the purposes of this document, the term "shared parenting" (also referred to as co-parenting) will be defined as both parents being meaningfully involved with their children and neither parent being able to make unilateral decisions, unless certain decisions have been delegated to them by the Court or by the other parent.

Thompson (2004) discussed refinements to the 1996 *Gordon v. Goertz* decision which identified primary caregivers as the parent who looks after the countless, essential, day-to-day tasks of parenting such as lunches, play dates, homework, clothing, appointments and the like.

Developmental Challenges Associated with Divorce

In general, children from divorced families have more adjustment difficulties than children from intact families, regardless of the custody arrangements (Dacey, Kenny and Margolis, 2000).

In addition, the phenomena referred to as the "sleeper effect" suggests that negative impacts of divorce on children may not become manifest until adolescence (Jaffe, 1998). Hayes (2010) stated multiple studies have demonstrated the negative effects of parental conflict on children. Fidler and Bala (2010) reported that when high-conflict parental behaviour is combined with child alienation, the risk to the well-being of the child is even greater. It is not the physical presence of one or two parents in the lives of the child that makes a difference; rather, it is the quality of interactions the child has with the parents they are involved with. In contrast, other authors state that children love, need and want both parents (Ricci, 1997). Children growing up in two-parent families can be significantly damaged if relationships are inappropriate or abusive with one or both parents. Adjustment difficulties that are possible for children of divorce include increased rates of drug and alcohol use, school and community behavioural problems, school performance difficulties, interpersonal relationship difficulties with members of the opposite sex, precocious sexual activity and a more negative view of marriage. As adults, children of divorce may experience lower levels of occupational attainment and higher rates of divorce (Steinberg, 2002).

Distance between parental homes is another factor to consider, as the normal development of teenagers includes them wishing to spend more time with peers and less time with parents; and having to move back and forth between neighbourhoods could be problematic (Trombetta, 1989). When parents live further apart from each other than a one-hour drive, the children do significantly less well emotionally and behaviourally than the children of divorce whose parents do not relocate (Palmer, 2003).

Some people believe that parents want shared parenting to minimise child support payments. However, this belief does not have any credible evidence to support it, nor does the belief in the need for a child to have a primary residence. Some research suggests that children who see one parent a few weekends per month experience the greatest sense of loss despite the "stability" of one residence (Holtzworth-Munroe, Applegate & D'Onofrio, 2009).

Children of divorced families, especially males, exhibit significantly more adjustment problems, such as acting out behaviours, and marital conflict in both intact and divorced families further erodes child adjustment (Kelly, 1993).

Isabella, et al (2003, p. 292) stated that fathers being absent or uninvolved strongly contributes to family instability, poverty and behavioural problems for the children.

One of the strongest contributors to the prevention of delinquent behaviour in children is consistent parental monitoring, which suggests the need for parents to work closely together in the raising and supervision of their children (Zahn, 2007).

Multiple factors and challenges exist for children during and following family break-up. Table 1 summarizes many of these factors.

Table 1: Potential Threats to Well Being in Children of Separation/Divorce
(Adapted from Nielsen, 1996; Jaffe, 1998: Elkind, 2001; Greenstone & Leviton, 2002).

- Depression, especially in response to parental adjustment to the separation.
- Lower standard of living and change in lifestyle/life opportunities.
- Prolonged exposure to parental conflict, prior to and following separation/divorce.

- Increase in general adjustment issues arising from multiple changes and transitions
- Lack of emotional availability in parents/absence of adequate parental support systems.
- Multiple family transitions.
- Separation of children from members of extended family.
- Children take on role of parent or partner or serve as a therapist or confidante.

Kelly (1993) states that children of divorce consistently describe the loss of contact with a parent as a negative event, but it may not significantly impact their overall adjustment. However, children with opposite-sex custodial parents tend to desire more contact with their same-sex parent. It has also been found that there is a relationship between consistent and frequent contact with the noncustodial parent and positive child adjustment, assuming that parent's behaviour was appropriate. Kelly (1993) also found that children with a father who was involved after separation did better in peer relationships and had higher achievement in mathematics and spelling. To a degree, positive behaviour in girls was also seen to be related to the amount of contact with their fathers.

Attachment Between Parent and Child

Attachment is seen to be a process and not a discrete event. When children enter into a divorce with close relationships with both parents, their adjustment will continue in a positive direction (Kelly, 1993).

Attachment is seen to be a process and not a discrete event.

Pruett, Ebling & Insabella (2004) indicate that children are capable of being meaningfully attached to both parents by six months of age and that the attachment depends on both child factors and the capabilities of the parents. The argument is made that it is not the amount of time parents and children spent together, but parents being involved in a variety of routine tasks including feeding, soothing and putting the children to bed, that strengthen and build relationships.

Catalysts for Dysfunction—Just Add Conflict and Stir

Conflict between parents is seen to lead to depression in children (Seligman, 1996). Interestingly, one study found that teachers could not determine if children were in split or in intact families based on their behaviour, although they could tell if the children came from a family that was harmonious or conflicted based on their behaviour (Jaffe, 1998).

Children are the "innocent bystanders" in often toxic battles between the two individuals to whom they are most attached. Such children are at "risk for a lifelong legacy of divorce, including higher rates of school dropout, out-of-wedlock pregnancy, marriage during adolescence, reduced life satisfaction and eventual disruption of their own marriages" (Peadro-Carroll, Nakhnikian & Montes, 2001, 377).

A premise behind shared parenting is the parents' ability to share. "Shared does not always mean equal, and unequal does not always mean unfair." (Taylor, 1989. p. 8).

Advantages of Shared Parenting

Many developmental advantages have been noted by having both a mother and a father significantly involved in the lives of the child. For example, it has been noted that when children have fathers appropriately involved in their lives, they are seen to be more mature and well-adjusted as adolescents. Father involvement has also been correlated with the development of empathy, achievement and later vocational success. Children raised in father-absent homes, especially boys, are more likely to behave more aggressively (Gould and Martindale, 2007). Mothers are seen to have a strong influence on how children interpret and understand their own behaviour and the behaviour of those around them, and mothers generally impact significantly on socialization (Nielsen, 1996). The point here is that both parents contribute to the child, although in slightly different fashions, and that it takes meaningful involvement from both parents to give the maximum opportunity for well-rounded development. In fairness, it has also been noted in parent-absent families that a stepparent or grandparent can provide some of the same benefits during the child's upbringing.

> The point here is that both parents
> contribute to the child...

It has also been noted that adolescents living in single-parent families or even in stepfamilies often are less well supervised than those in intact families (Jaffe, 1998).

Even within families going through amicable splits, one child can flounder while another flourishes. Children under stress are more prone to mental health disorders (Pearce &

Pezzot-Pearce, 1997), and parents can play a pivotal role in the development of resiliency in children (Fleming, 2002).

Multiple threats to adjustment and resilience exist within the context of a family going through separation or divorce. The majority of these relate to the mental health and behaviours of the parents (Nielsen, 1996; Jaffe, 1998: Elkind, 2001). Professionals must also take some responsibility with the provision of appropriate, timely services and interventions to minimise the length of uncertainty that children face.

Parent-child attachments are formed through interaction between the parent and child. The notion that a child can only attach to one caregiver has been disproven. However, to form attachments, children require meaningful and frequent contact with parental figures in a variety of situations (Gould and Martindale, 2007). In the absence of interactions in a variety of contexts, parent-child relationships are likely to weaken and are difficult to re-establish once disrupted. It is best for young children to have continuity in their relationships with their parents and to minimize or prevent disruptions from ever taking place (Kelly and Lamb, 2000, 2003).

Children need protection from parental conflict and litigation. Early and decisive intervention needs to take place to stop potential alienation before it becomes established (Jaffe, Ashbourne & Mamo, 2010). Jaffe et al (2010) note that in high-conflict, established cases of alienation, there is a lack of evidence that simply terminating contact between the child and alienating parent, and providing intensive therapy with the estranged parent and the child, is beneficial, as the child's security and stability are removed.

From a parent's perspective, a major advantage of shared parenting is that it allows each parent time off from parental responsibilities (Taylor, 1998).

Kelly (1993) described a variety of research findings with respect to joint custody:

- Children report being more satisfied when in joint custody situations due to keeping a close relationship with both parents.

- Most children do not report being confused or having loyalty issues with joint custody situations.

- Parents acknowledge relying on one another in joint custody situations and report that joint custody enhances relationships between the child and the parents.

- When children reside with both parents, each parent reports more time to play or have conversation with their children.

- In joint custody, fathers are seen to have higher involvement with their children.

- Adolescents who reside only with their fathers may not be as well adjusted as those who alternate between parents or who reside with their mothers.

Specific visitation schedules, whether court-ordered or prepared by parents, provide greater predictability, create mutually binding expectations and add stability to co-parenting patterns following separation or divorce (Hirczy de Mino, 1997).

When parents provide child care in a coordinated manner, with similar routines and schedules, children are seen to do better behaviourally and socially (Pruett, et al, 2004).

Disadvantages of Shared Parenting

With shared parenting, clearly defined and mutually accepted guidelines and processes are required, whether parenting time or child support, because it is normal for parents to think selfishly about their children (Maida, 1997). In addition, regulations such as child support guidelines give the clear message to parents that they are both responsible for supporting their children.

Shared parenting by itself may not be the solution to all developmental challenges faced by children in divorced families. Early studies found that custody arrangements by themselves are not significant predictors of child adjustment and that other factors also need to be considered (Kelly, 1993).

Shared parenting on paper can be quite different from shared parenting in practice. It has been indicated repeatedly that Family Courts are directing shared custody and residence for children, although the fathers are often seen to be the non-resident parent (Finley and Schwartz, 2010). Emerging "21st century issues" include father's rights in unmarried families (Moulton, 2009) and recognizing the rights of the non-biological parent in families with same sex parents (Miller, 2011).

While *false* allegations do take place in divorce, so do *true* allegations.

For many divorced families, especially initially, the concept of shared parenting is not either desirable or immediately achievable. The ability to co-parent must be viewed as a skill, one which parents who have just gone through an often emotional breakup need to learn (Garon, Donner and Peacock, 2000). **The task for such families is to do their divorce better than they did their marriage.** Successfully learning to communicate and co-parent may be one of the most important parenting tasks they can undertake. According to Garon, et al. (2000), the large majority of researchers, mental health practitioners, parents and children agree that both parents should be meaningfully involved with their children. Following this assumption, battles for sole custody are not in a child's best interests. What children need is to benefit from what both parents have to offer.

Shared parenting can prolong parental conflict in the case of parents who neither have the inclination or the skills to learn to work together (McIntosh, 2009).

A cautious approach needs to be taken when domestic violence is present. While violence often ends with the physical separation of the parents, ongoing spousal abuse can still take place and in extreme cases issues of life or death exist. While *false* allegations do take place in divorce, so do *true* allegations. Allegations can be difficult to prove, as much of the behaviours constituting domestic violence take place behind closed doors and go un-witnessed (Jaffe, Johnston, Crooks & Bala, 2008). Jaffe et al (2008) state that co-parenting is not appropriate for cases with domestic violence, especially cases involving "chronic conflict, coercive interactions, inability to jointly problem solve, no history of capacity to cooperate or communicate" (p. 511) or when untreated mental illness or substance abuse exists.

Conclusions

Two major areas of concern arise in examining the importance of both parents being meaningfully involved in the upbringing of their children: parental absence and parental conflict. Both situations are created out of the selfishness of parents and the inability of them to put the needs of the children ahead of their own needs. Remarkably, many high-conflict parents are seen to be highly functional in all other aspects of life except when dealing with their ex-partner. Parental absence has clearly been associated with developmental (emotional, social and behavioural) disturbances for the children. Parental absence can be unavoidable in the case of death; unfortunate in the case of the parent who does not want to be involved; and preventable in the case of one parent trying to eliminate the other parent from the child's life. Parental conflict, whether within the marriage or after the divorce, has also been found to create multiple developmental difficulties for the children.

Attachment research shows that children are able to form multiple meaningful bonds, although those bonds are created and maintained by predictable and frequent contact with parenting figures. Such bonds can be damaged or broken through extended absences and are maintained through consistent and appropriate parenting, where the parental figure engages in a wide variety of routine tasks with the child as opposed to only being involved with play-time weekends.

Distance between homes and parental communication and cooperation are key factors for success.

Some court custody decisions have been based on a view that if there is a high level of conflict there should be a primary parent, and minimal contact and communication between the parents, in an effort to reduce the children's exposure to conflict. This is at best a Band-Aid solution that allows misbehaving and selfish parents to take control and inflict damage on their children through both the creation of conflict and exclusion of the other parent. Such a decision does not take into account the abundant research of the benefits for children to have both parents involved or the ability for conflict to be reduced with proper counselling for the family.

Shared parenting does not equate to each parent having exactly 26 weeks per year or 3½ days per week. In many American jurisdictions the "approximation rule" is considered. The "approximation rule" looks at parental time and involvement pre-divorce and equates that with post-divorce parenting time. A significant flaw in this approach is that married families often specialize: the parent with the greatest earning power spends more time working and the other parent spends more time in child rearing activities. As a result divorced families require significant restructuring.

Families always have the three resources of time, energy and money. Divorced families need to restructure how such resources are utilized. **Clearly, being the sole parent during parenting time is more labour-intensive than having two adults involved at any given time with the children.** Having two households is more expensive than sharing one. Divorced families out of necessity require both parents to become generalists to a greater degree than previously seen and the children will benefit from significant and appropriate involvement by both parents.

The one flaw that can occur in shared parenting is when parents treat their children as possessions, or worse, wanting time with the children primarily to punish the other parent. From a child's perspective, there is nothing that makes sense about having to be in a daycare setting during their time with "parent one" because that parent is at work, while "parent two" may be available to provide care at that time.

The ideal for optimal positive child development is for the parents to cooperate and communicate in developing a schedule that makes sense based on their expertise and availability. This allows the child maximal exposure to parental strengths and the experience of routine and stability in each home. As a final note, when families have more than one child, exemplary co-parenting also provides for one-on-one time between each child and each parent.

Information on Bonding

For purposes of this book the terms "bonding" and "attachment" are used synonymously.

A historic legal opinion by the Supreme Court of Pennsylvania in 1813 created the *tender age* viewpoint which said that young children need care and assistance that is best provided by a mother. Around this time a British barrister expressed the idea that the mother should have care of the child until the age of 7 and the father should have custody of the child after the age of 7. (Gould, 2006). This viewpoint became known as the *tender years doctrine*.

The development of theories of attachment by researchers such as Bowlby (1969, 1980) provided a research basis for parent-child relationships contrasting with the earlier opinion-based views. Gould (2006) reported that research has shown infants are capable of forming strong attachments to both parents by approximately six months of age, although this research is only beginning to influence the tender years/maternal preference of the Courts. Further, infants are capable of strong attachments to primary caretakers and can experience behavioural and emotional regression, depression and a profound sense of loss when separated from those caretakers.

Developmental psychologist Erik Erikson focused on factors leading to the development of a healthy personality in children. Erikson indicated that the task of the newborn is to learn to trust the primary caregivers during the first year of life and if this task is interrupted or not accomplished, subsequent stages will not develop accordingly and difficulties can occur throughout the lifespan for such individuals (Thomas, 1985). Recent research specifically related to custody and access issues states that one of the most significant accomplishments of the newborn child during the first year is to develop attachments to parents and caregivers (Kelly & Lamb, 2000). The strength of parent-child bonding is further described by Thomas (1985) as a strong two-way attachment between the child and caregiver that can continue even if the caregiver is later harsh or inappropriate.

Infants who receive responsive and sensitive care from familiar adults through tasks such as feeding, playing and soothing become securely attached to those caregivers (Kelly & Lamb, 2000). Children are further seen to be better off with insecure attachments, created by only adequate levels of "parental" responsiveness, than they are without attachments at all.

From birth to approximately two months of age the infant is just starting to recognize caregiver facial expression and sounds. For about the following six months infants are recognizing and more easily soothed by primary caregivers.

This stage is also the earliest beginnings of trust developing in the infant's relationship with the parent. Research is increasingly demonstrating that infants have meaningful attachments to both parents by approximately 7 months of age, even though one parent often spends more time with the child than the other. Once these attachments are formed, the infant will seek out these primary attachment figures for nurturing and soothing. While an infant may show some preference for the parent they spend the most time with, this preference becomes negligible by the age of 18 months (Kelly and Lamb (2000).

With respect to disrupted attachments, Kelly and Lamb (2000) indicate that attachments need ongoing nurturing through contact with both parents and that lengthy separations from either parent can be damaging to attachments. Additionally, parent-child contact should represent a variety of parent-child activities, including nurturing, feeding and soothing, and should not just be structured play time. Eliminating one parent from a child's life may damage the attachment and re-establishing a bond may be difficult.

While many studies of attachment initially focused on mother-child relationships, it has long been known that fathers also play a unique and important role in attachments with their children. Infants, during their first year, are seen to form distinct attachments to both parents despite tending to have a greater level of interaction with their mothers. In fact, there can be more attachment figures for infants than just the two parents, although when stressed children tend to need nurturing from one of their close attachment figures (Ludolph, 2009).

In the past it was thought that once a child attached to a parental figure he or she maintained this attachment over time. More recently it has been noted that this is only the case when the child experiences reasonably stable family conditions during their first two years of life (Kelly and Lamb, 2000). Relegating one parent to infrequent access with the child is misuse of Bowlby's earliest works that initially speculated that a child could only have one primary attachment; a notion which has been disproven since that time. More transitions, rather than fewer, are required in order to be responsive to an infant's psychological needs.

Many researchers indicate the need for both mothers and fathers to be meaningfully involved in the upbringing of their children, and the long-term mental health benefits for the children when involved with appropriate, nurturing parents (for example, Braver, Griffin and Cookston, 2005).

Bonding/attachment is not only an infant concept, but is important for adolescents. Those with secure parental attachments are more likely able to have secure peer (and romantic) attachments. Findley and Schwartz (2010) speak of the problems for children of conflicted divorce. They point out that children in intact families live in one primary system while children of divorce must adapt to each parent occupying a different world. Having the family in two different worlds can have long-term negative impact on the psychosocial adjustment of the child.

While there are still some authors who maintain that children under the age of three should sleep in the same home every night, an increasing majority of authors in this area, who are informed by current research in child development, see no reason for such a restriction (Warshak, 2000). In fact, the ability of both parents to provide a "full range" of care giving activities for the child is seen to be a bonus in developing secure attachments for the child. It has been noted that most preschool children are prone to exhibit some distress when separated from either parent (aside from unique events such as vacations) for more than three or four days. Warshak (2007) identifies the risks of the "approximation rule," in which parents are granted post-divorce time and involvement with the children in the same ratio as their pre-divorce involvement, as ignoring the child's needs and their previous experience of the family when it was intact.

Within the field of developmental psychology there is a need for more research regarding father-child attachment (Lee, Kaufman and George, 2007) and the need for validation of some of the measures/instruments used to determine attachment (Ludolph, 2009).

Weighing against the benefits of the child developing and maintaining multiple attachments is the risk of damage caused by parental conflict (Johnson, 1995; Gould, 2006; Kelly, 1993). Unfortunately, this dilemma has been addressed by some courts by making the unfortunate statement that joint custody should not exist in high-conflict situations. The flip side to this situation, which appears more in the developmental interest of the child, is that parents who willingly enter into conflict with the other parent are being selfish, if not abusive, and need to be dealt with accordingly.

Ethical Issues

Knowledge and Skill Base

Family Restructuring Therapy requires the mental health professional to have specialized knowledge in the areas of child development, family systems, divorce, grief and loss, working with the legal system, and personality and emotional difficulties. The therapist should have experience working with children of all ages (including teenagers), with individual counselling, and working with couples and families. The family law system has its own culture, language and pitfalls that is different from that of criminal law or even from child protection issues.

Limitations

Family Restructuring Therapy is a therapeutic process, not a form of assessment. A therapist should <u>never</u> make recommendations regarding custody and/or access without doing a full custody assessment. I often see therapists getting themselves into difficulty with regulatory bodies or boards for making statements such as "the child appears genuinely frightened of their parent and should not have to spend time with that parent until a full assessment is done". The therapist ignores professional ethics to put forward client concerns and in doing so deems a parent unsafe, at times without even having seen this parent. This can significantly impact a family law case, relationships between the parents, and relationships between the children and parents. I may be good at doing assessments myself, but I still have not figured out the trick of assessing a person that I have not met.

A therapist should <u>never</u> make recommendations regarding custody and/or access without doing a full custody assessment.

Of course, professional ethical guidelines still apply regarding the concepts of duty to protect a child from harm/abuse or a person from self-harm, and the duty to warn others of potential harm to themselves still applies. Professionals should be very knowledgeable about the guidelines and standards that apply in their own jurisdictions.

Despite the limitation of not making recommendations, Family Restructuring Therapy is an open process, meaning that any information/observation made by the therapist can be reported to the court. In this case, the report is narrative, not evaluative, and gives the Court a picture of the family and children that cannot be seen in Court. If you do make any "recommendations," only include things both parents could benefit from, as an assessment was not done. However, the first time I did such a narrative report, I felt guilty that I was not really saying anything, given my extensive background as an assessor. I was in the fortunate position of being able to speak to the case management judge on the case. I stated my concern that the report was somewhat wishy-washy. The judge replied, "Oh no, Steve, the information is all there, it's right between the lines."

It is this accountability that gives Family Restructuring Therapy its strength. Working with high-conflict families, a closed process that does not allow such a factual report to the Court can serve to escalate elevated conflict rather than to rein it in.

Multiple/Dual Roles

A common mistake therapists make in working with divorced families is taking on more than one role. A therapist cannot see both parents individually for counselling, see them jointly, see them with their children and see the children individually. Now let's review some possible ways that things can be done in an ethical manner.

The most common situation is one therapist working with the parents only. In this case, I see each parent one time individually. This allows me to get an understanding of the situation from each parent's perspective without having the other parent in the room. It also gives me the chance to offer some individual pointers of what that parent might try differently to keep from falling into the trap of doing the same thing over and over with equally unsuccessful results. After these initial meetings, all contact takes place with both parents together only. This means:

- I will not take a phone call from one parent;
- if one parent does not show up for the appointment, I do not talk to the other parent alone;
- that I do not respond to emails unless they are also copied to the other parent.

If children of the relationship are in need of counselling, I refer them to a different therapist rather than trying to work with the parents and children in different combinations. If I am the person working with the child, I do not have one-sided communications with either parent, which could inadvertently escalate custody battles. Instead, communication takes place with the parents jointly, or, if they are also in counselling, with their individual therapists (after the appropriate consents are signed).

The same principles also apply regarding contact with lawyers for either party. Additionally, if you are in the role of therapist in the case, you cannot do anything pertaining to other aspects of the same case, such as evaluating another mental health professional's work or conducting an assessment of any of the family members.

Informed Consent

Informed consent is an important aspect of the process of Family Restructuring Therapy. I always start by clarifying role expectations with all parties involved, explaining the process and limits of confidentiality, and providing a retainer letter also outlining this information. **When working with children of divorce, I insist on having one of the following: consent of both parents, proof of sole custody from the parent bringing the child to see me, or a court order directing counselling for that child.** Keep in mind that informed consent does not simply mean providing a document outlining the process, but ensuring that each participant understands the process, limitations and confidentiality in a language that he or she can understand. This applies to children as well as parents.

As stated previously, I cannot emphasize enough that you become very familiar with the laws, rules, guidelines and policies in your jurisdiction, whether you believe you are involved in the family law system or not. The potential is high that you will become involved at some point in your career in a family law case, whether you want to or not, and whether you intend to or not.

CHAPTER 3

Legal Issues

Legal Issues

Family Restructuring Therapy is often court-directed, but parents can be referred by counsel or even self-referred.

Family Restructuring Therapy can take place pre-settlement or post-settlement, and in fact can be a useful process to head off more intrusive interventions such as a custody assessment or evaluation.

If there are significant, unproven allegations (abuse, violence, alcohol/drug abuse), then Family Restructuring Therapy is <u>not</u> the appropriate process and an assessment and/or a trial is likely a better alternative.

> In my view, cooperation and litigation cannot co-exist.

Family Restructuring Therapy is an open process. In my jurisdiction, a referral may come directly from the court that also allows the therapist to communicate with the case management judge.

As a requirement for me to work with families, I include a statement in my retainer letter that neither party can engage in any applications to the court (notice of motion, filing of affidavits, etc.) while I am working with them. In my view, cooperation and litigation cannot co-exist.

Depending on the situation, mental health professionals may want a court order appointing them and also allowing them to limit access by the parents or their counsel to any material obtained during Family Restructuring Therapy. If you are going to write letters and release information, you should clarify this in advance in the retainer agreement.

The therapist's best protection (aside from competence) is a detailed and clear retainer agreement designed to meet the unique and specific needs of the family.

I hope you weren't expecting a long section on legal issues. I am a psychologist, not a lawyer.

Therapist Characteristics

Well, you have read this far, or perhaps started with this chapter, and are wondering if you are suited for this kind of work. I have included a list of characteristics needed by therapists to work in this field. The main two characteristics are experience and confidence. When I work in this area I tend to be blunt, use humour to turn examples into caricatures for emphasis and tell clients the rules right up front. If they don't play nicely I will ask them to leave. In our office, the other extreme is Dr. Bonnie Haave who comes across in such a positive and friendly manner that clients don't dare misbehave out of the fear of offending her. In between are our other partners, Dr. Shirley Vandersteen and Mr. Jim Bateman, who have a mixture that is best described as "firm but fair."

First, the therapist must be genuine, using his or her own approaches, interventions and personality.

In short, there is a key difference between Family Restructuring Therapy and other models of working with divorced families. First, the therapist must be genuine, using his or her own approaches, interventions and personality. Second, as we will discuss later, the approach must be modified to meet the unique needs of each family individually. There is no uniform cookie-cutter approach that can be applied to all families.

Therapist characteristics include:
1. Possess expert knowledge in child development, family dynamics, communication, grief and loss, separation and divorce, and child protection issues.
2. The ability to tightly control and direct therapy sessions.
3. The ability to engage and lead the family while being firmly in control of the family system.
4. The ability to prescribe and teach functional skills, behaviours, and relationship transactions.

The specific tasks the therapist needs to do during the sessions include:
1. To prevent escalation of conflict by dealing with conflict or unacceptable/rude behaviour as it occurs; by teaching positive behaviours; and being willing to stop the session if necessary.
2. To shift the focus from the positions of the parents to the underlying needs of each member of the family.
3. To ensure that primary consideration is given to the needs of the child.
4. To protect the child and validate his or her initial views, while moving the child forward to accept appropriate parental authority.
5. To remain disengaged from the family and avoid getting caught in the conflict.

6. To model appropriate behaviour by showing respect to the family members in an appropriate "business-like" way.

7. To recognize the functional strengths of the parents in other areas of their lives.

8. To engage the parent's strengths in making the required changes to meet the needs of their child.

9. To teach parents the skills and behaviours required to co-parent, to re-establish a healthy relationship with the child and to build a functional parenting plan.

CHAPTER 5

High-Conflict Parents and
High-Conflict Children

High-Conflict Parents

High-conflict parents live in imaginary boxes. **For the high-conflict parent, there are only two boxes in life: *with me* or *against me*.** Although these parents have their own negative history and state they do not want their own children to experience what they did, they often cannot see their own behaviour clearly enough to recognize it and learn to change it without assistance. Some of these parents are honest enough and have enough insight that they will actually tell you, "I know my behaviour doesn't make sense, but I want the other person to hurt as bad as I have been hurt". Others may have significant issues that they need to first or concurrently address in intensive personal therapy. Bill Eddy, in his book *High Conflict People in Legal Disputes* (Eddy, 2008), describes many of these people as having personality disorders. This is often true of the person who starts the conflict, but even if the other individual does not by nature have a high-conflict personality, he or she may resort to high-conflict tactics in an attempt to fight fire with fire.

Some parents appear as high-conflict personalities in all matters pertaining to the other parent, but are otherwise well-functioning in all other areas of life.

High-conflict parents do not suddenly appear. They tend to have a long history of relationship conflicts that can include childhood abuse or disrupted early childhood relationships. As high-conflict is nothing new in divorce settings, a personal history of being a child of a conflicted divorce can also be found in many cases. Such individuals often have an adversarial view of relationships, they lack insight and are unable to accept loss or heal from it. Keep in mind that normal grieving processes can be significantly extended in divorce situations. Often, the person who finally ends the relationship has been going through preparatory grief for months or years before leaving. The person who has been left then starts their own grieving process which can also take a significant time. This leaves the family unit chaotic and disorganized for an extended period.

High-conflict parents do not suddenly appear.

High-conflict parents blame others for the conflict and the problems. It is always someone else's fault. As they have been wronged, their goal is to win and winning can include custody, assets, affection of the child or imaginary contests. **There is a need to be right and more importantly to prove that the other person is wrong or bad.** In a quest to destroy the other parent, forgiveness is not possible and such individuals justify their behaviour even if it is hurtful to the child. In many cases, you will find it puzzling that people who are otherwise excellent parents engage in behaviours that are so harmful to their children without noticing it. Therefore, a key component of

Family Restructuring Therapy is to make the parents explicitly aware of the damage they are doing to the children involved.

The term "narcissistic rage" has often been used to describe some high-conflict parents. Such parents, while generally logical individuals, can engage in some illogical, immoral and even illegal acts. The high-conflict parent believes that the other parent does not even deserve to exist, let alone have a part in their child's life. Some parents will actually produce a list of all the faults and wrongdoings of the other parent.

The most difficult aspect of the high-conflict parents is a profound lack of insight they have into what the conflict is doing to the children, and blame is always deflected to the other parent.

High-Conflict Children

Like in any other area of family dysfunction, some children are resilient and survive horrendous parental conflict, while others are significantly troubled by even minor conflict. The example I often use is of a preteen girl who academically stated, "Genetically, I am 50% my mother. Since my father hates my mother that part of me must be bad. I am also 50% genetically my father. Since my mother hates my father there goes the other half. I must be all bad so what does it matter if I cut myself?"

While most children in conflict-free divorced or intact families try to play one parent against the other, children of high-conflict divorce can turn this into an art form. The reason they are so good at it is simple survival. While children often are not able to verbalize what is going on inside of them, it can be described as "Mom (or dad) threw away dad (or mom), so if I'm not careful they can throw me away too. I need to show them that I'm on their side so they don't get rid of me." Children will often be over-questioned or inappropriately questioned upon return from the other parent's home and it appears that the questioning parent is not happy until they hear something negative. To adapt, the children will tell negative things, true or not, as their admission back into the home. The same parent who would not believe the child if they came home on Monday from school saying, "The teacher said because it is going to be so nice out all week we can take the rest of the week off", often believes even more ridiculous statements made by the child about the other parent.

Children often show rejecting behaviour towards one parent that can be summarized by the "four A's" of rejection.

The first A is "alienation", the child being turned against one parent. This can be done deliberately by a parent, grandparent, sibling or other influential individual making negative statements (true or fabricated) about the other parent. This can take place accidentally when children, being inherently somewhat nosy, listen in on conversations and try to obtain "the truth" about what is going on. The same child who does not appear to hear a parent asking loudly for him to empty the dishwasher can instantly zero in on the parent speaking in another room on the telephone in a quiet voice.

The second A is "alignment", the tendency of a child to choose one side in a high-conflict divorce. This is strictly a survival method, because for some children it is easier to pick one parent and eliminate the other than it is to feel constantly torn between two people they love. Sometimes the child will pick the parent who has been hurt, out of the belief that she needs to help that parent. Other times, the child will pick the dominant/aggressive parent to keep that parent from turning his or her wrath on the child.

The third A is "attachment", in that at different times in the child's life, based on their emotional needs, interests and temperament, he may feel closer to one parent or another for a variety of healthy and appropriate reasons. The sports star child may have more in common with an athletic parent, while a creative child may have more in common with an artistic parent.

The fourth A is "appropriate", where a child is appropriately disconnected from an inappropriate parent, due to negative experiences with that parent in the past either directed towards the child or that the child witnessed between the parent and the other parent or a sibling.

Other aspects of high-conflict children pertain to false allegations. False allegations can become part of the child's personal history if she grows to believe the allegations are true. At this point, from the child's perspective, it does not matter whether she was abused, or just convinced that she was abused, as she now believes it to be true. Therefore, a parent who creates false allegations needs to be viewed as just as abusive as an actual abusive parent. Along with this, children can be enlisted into a parent's dysfunctional behaviour. It is this dynamic that leads a 10-year-old boy to scream from the window of the vilified parent's home, "Help! I've been kidnapped by a child abuser", to passerby's on the street.

The high-conflict child takes up
one parent's cause

The high-conflict child learns negative and rude behaviours by watching his parents interact. Once a child is shown that such inappropriate behaviour is okay, because his parents treat each other that way, the child learns to act this way toward other adults, such as teachers, resulting in negative consequences. A child becomes insecure as he views one or both parents as bad; therefore, who can he trust? In addition, if a child is empowered to behave negatively towards one parent, he may soon generalize that he can treat both parents in such a manner.

The high-conflict child takes up one parent's cause and this can often be seen in her language by her frequent use of the word "us" or "we", by showing knowledge of adult issues and by using terminology that surpasses her understanding. The high-conflict parent will maintain that the child has a right to know or must be warned for the child's own safety. The high-conflict child when discussing her problem with the rejected parent will often describe a single issue over and over again to explain all her problems. An example of this is the 13-year-old girl explaining that the other parent could not be trusted because when she was 7 years old she was promised a pony ride for her birthday that never took place, with this being the only concrete example of wrongdoing that could be described. When all else fails, the high-conflict child relies on the standby phrase, "I just don't feel safe."

A key point of Family Restructuring Therapy is that while it focuses on the child's perspective and needs, and children are allowed to express opinions, they are not allowed to make decisions about significant aspects of their lives. There is a valid reason why children are not able to drive a car until 16, vote until the age of 18 or drink until the ages of 18, 19 or 21 depending where they live. **Unfortunately, the "Myth of 12" exists in some locations where courts give strong consideration to what a child as young as 12 years old wants. There is no aspect of child development that would suggest a 12-year-old has the intellectual development, social development, moral development or development in any other area that**

would allow her to knowledgeably make such a decision. If adults allow a 12-year-old to reject one parent in favour of the other, it follows that this 12-year-old should also be able to make choices about skipping school, getting tattoos, doing alcohol or drugs, or engaging in sexual behaviour. Of course, any of these could lead to disastrous consequences for the child, as could being supported to reject one parent.

PART II

Processes of Family Resturcturing Therapy

CHAPTER 6

Working With the Parents

The most common process in Family Restructuring Therapy is one therapist working with two parents. These cases can be self-referred and not include legal counsel; they can be referred by counsel pre-or post-judgment or referred by the court. The cases referred by counsel or the court are almost exclusively high-conflict cases and even here a distinction needs to be made. If it is a "normal" high-conflict case with multiple court appearances, a prolonged battle and other factors of concern, there is the possibility of working with a single therapist. If it is an extreme case where there have been significant behavioural outbursts by the parents even in a structured setting such as a court room, if restraining orders are in place or other extreme factors (such as a history of mutual violence towards each other) exist, it is more advisable to have two therapists conducting the Family Restructuring Therapy. One who works with one of the parents, and the other who works with the other parent and who both take part in joint sessions. Either way, the process of Family Restructuring Therapy follows a similar pattern, with the exception that in a two therapist process individual sessions with each parent and his or her therapist can take place throughout the process on an as-needed basis.

The starting point is having a brief meeting, usually a telephone conference call, with both lawyers to establish the appropriateness of the process, what the process will look like and who is responsible for payment. After this, the therapist produces a retainer letter sent to both lawyers. This process can be done with self-represented parties, although the need for advanced discussion and the production of a retainer agreement cannot be by-passed.

A. The Retainer Letter
A typical retainer letter will have the following components:

Sample Retainer Letter
Family Restructuring Therapy
Smith & Wesson
December 21, 2012

> **Explanation :**
> Like anything else, the retainer begins with the title. One important part here is to put an "and" between the parents names rather than a "versus" as this is a collaborative process, not litigiousness one. Including the date is important as it will also later help identify if one party or the other is trying to stall the process.

Family Restructuring Therapy is an active, directive process with families in conflict to modify maladaptive interactions. This therapy can be used for teaching parents to co-parent and in developing concrete, practical parenting plans.

Explanation:

A generic introductory paragraph that describes what the process is. You may need to modify this based on the specific goals set out in your opening conference. Whether parents like it or not I continue to refer to them as a family, as the family is from the child's perspective (having two parents) and not from the parent's perspective of being divorced.

Referral:

Smith and Wesson were referred for Family Restructuring Therapy by their counsel. The initial goals were described as assisting these parents in communicating effectively and to help them design a parenting plan that will address developmentally appropriate changes in parenting time for the children, extracurricular activities and processes for vacations. Other goals will be set out by the parents themselves in the initial sessions.

Explanation :

In this section the referral goals are outlined in more detail and where the referral came from is mentioned. It is important to describe clearly what is to be worked on as this document will be the basis of informed consent when you first meet with the parents.

Limitations:

This process is not a custody assessment and no opinions can be given regarding custody and/or access. It is assumed that in this process the parents are working towards meaningful and appropriate contact between the children and their parents and developing a parenting plan that meets the specific needs of the children.

Explanation :

It is common that those in the legal system misunderstand the process and limitations of Family Restructuring Therapy and are actually looking for a "bargain basement" custody assessment. It is important to spell out clearly, in advance that this is a therapeutic process, not an assessment, and that no recommendations can be made regarding custody or access.

If you look at local, national or international guidelines for Child Custody Assessment, all well thought out guidelines will tell you that, in making custody recommendations, it is essential to assess all family members, examine their relationships, strengths and weaknesses and conduct collateral contacts and observations (at a minimum).

To make a statement regarding custody or access (parenting time) you are in fact giving custody recommendations without conducting an assessment.

Confidentiality:

This is an open process meaning that any information obtained during work with the family may be used by the therapist, at her/his discretion, in a report that will be provided to (the Court, both parties through their counsel) at (the therapist's discretion, the request of the Court, after 10 sessions). No information can be provided that will be considered "off the record". This includes comments made or behaviours observed during the session, in the waiting room, information in e-mails between the parents, information on attendance and punctuality or pertaining to payment of retainer.

If either of the children (Kim or Jordan) are seen to require individual counselling separate therapist(s) will be assigned for them and the parents will not have direct contact with either therapist. The therapist working with the parents will have permission to contact the child's therapist(s) and all information will flow between them.

Explanation :

It is essential to state in the letter that this is an open process in that any information obtained by the therapist during the process of conducting Family Restructuring Therapy could be provided by a letter to the court or to counsel for both parties. This is one of the strengths of this process in that bad behaviour or a lack of cooperation cannot be hidden.

While the therapist is not doing an assessment, a detailed narrative report of what was said, done and attempted can provide valuable information to the Court should the therapeutic process fail.

Sometimes, the most revealing observations are those made pre-or post session as the parents enter or leave the office.

It is also essential that the therapist working with the parents is able to speak with the individual(s) working with children. This is a good way to gather information that is in dispute between the parents and to find out how the children feel on a variety of topics.

Informed consent and confidentiality applies to all participants. The children should be aware, in advance, how any of their statements could be utilized or how they could be communicated to their parents.

Process:

- Pat Smith will be seen for an initial one-hour individual session.
- Kelly Wesson will be seen for a one hour individual session.
- All further sessions involving the parents will be joint with no one-sided contact (telephone, e-mail, face-to-face, etc.) allowed after the individual first sessions.
- The initial retainer will be for 12 hours: 2 hours for individual sessions, 8 hours for joint sessions and 2 hours for report writing (if necessary).
- At the end of the initial 10 hours of service a recommendation for further sessions will either be made or a report provided outlining progress and difficulties to date.
- If either of the children Kim or Jordan are seen to require counselling additional therapists will be assigned to work with them and additional retainer funds will be required.

Explanation :

It is important to outline what the sessions will actually look like so that first of all both parents understand the session begins with individual time for each of them. It is also made clear that all subsequent sessions will involve both parents and that they will in fact be in the same room for these meetings and that there is no one-sided contact allowed once the process begins. This prevents one parent from lobbying or trying to gain the sympathy of the therapist and further emphasizes neutrality/balance of the process.

If necessary a separate therapist can work with the children. If the children are similar in their relationships within the family and responses to the divorce one person can see them both although it is strongly recommended that the children have individual sessions to keep them from influencing each other. At other times, or in highly conflicted files, it is more prudent for each child to have their own therapist.

When you look at it if the total process took 14 hours for the parents, 6 hours for one child and 10 hours for the other it still works out to a total of 30 hours no matter how many therapists are involved. By having multiple therapists who can communicate with one another it minimizes the risk of role conflict within the file. Much damage has been done to divorced families by well-meaning people who tried to be everything for everyone and ended up making things worse.

Costs:

All services are billed at $ (your forensic rate) per hour. An initial retainer for 12 hours is required prior to the start of the process. If progress is being made and additional sessions are required a request for a further retainer will be made.

All activities related to this case (direct client contact, telephone and e-mail contact, communication with counsel or the Court, reporting, etc.) are considered to be billable time.

There is a 48-hour cancellation policy. Sessions missed or cancelled within 48 hours will be billed to the retainer. For joint sessions both parties must attend or the session will be listed as a missed appointment.

It is understood that Kelly Weston and Pat Smith are each responsible for paying 50% of the retainer.

Time for court appearances must be booked a minimum of 3 weeks in advance and a minimum cancellation time of 72 hours is required to prevent billing.

Explanation :

Simply put, this work isn't enough fun to do for free (not counting pro bono work that you engage in). The rationale for using a forensic rate—if this is part of your standard practice—is that there is much more of a nuisance factor with having to communicate, at times frequently, with counsel for the parties or the court. This is not work for the novice and a higher level of knowledge is expected with a high likelihood of having to describe your work in court if the outcome is not successful. In addition, while I indicate that emails, phone calls, etc. can be billed for I rarely do this. For example on a given day I might quickly scan 15 emails from 10 different families I am working with (and monitoring the communication between the parents) but I rarely need to take any more action than printing out a particular e-mail to address with the parents at a subsequent session.

I do not just bill the party who missed, but deduct the fee from the retainer and leave it for the parents and their lawyers to work it out at a later time.

Other:

As cooperation and litigation cannot co-exist it is expected that neither party will make any Court applications once engaged in Family Restructuring Therapy without the advance permission of the therapist.

It is expected that both parties will behave in a cordial manner during sessions and if their behaviour becomes inappropriate during a session that session can be terminated early at the therapist's discretion.

Explanation :

It is unrealistic to think that parents are able to put their full effort into learning to work together if they are also at war outside of the office. I recently had a request for doing Family Restructuring Therapy at the same time as the parents participating with a different psychologist in an open custody assessment. I politely but firmly declined to work with this family stating that they could either be in a therapeutic process with me or doing a custody assessment with the other psychologist, but not both.

I clearly tell the parents that while they remain in charge of parenting decisions I am in charge of the parenting communication within my office and that my office is a safe place. I reserve the right to be able to warn the parent(s) once to de-escalate inappropriate behaviour and that on the second occasion the session will be over for that day, but the process will continue at the next appointment. The parents need to know that they will be safe in the office and that there are strict limits to how they may act towards one another. I have not had to do this often as a lesson I learned long ago in a previous career as a junior high teacher, if you set the expectations clearly and in advance things tend to go far better.

Commencement of Services:

Once the retainer fee is provided the process can begin. Each parent's attendance at their initial appointment shall signify their agreement with the process.

Explanation :

Different cases may require different processes. For example, you may request to be court-appointed before starting. You may have a signed signature page that you want parents and their counsel to sign prior to starting or you can simply state that once the parents show up for their first appointment it is a sign that they are willing to participate.

B. The First Individual Sessions

All first sessions begin exactly the same. Parents are shown the retainer letter and asked if they have seen it in advance or if it has been communicated to them. Quite often the answer will be no. Regardless, I read over the entire retainer agreement with the parent, answer any questions he or she may have, and record in my notes that the process and confidentiality has been discussed and that the parent agreed to proceed. Once in awhile, parents will indicate they thought this was a custody assessment or that this would evaluate allegations of inappropriate parenting. After discussing the process with the parents, emphasizing what can and cannot be done, if they maintain it is the wrong process for them, a further letter is written to counsel for both parties (and/or the court) and the process is placed on hold.

The next portion of the first session is for the parents to describe all the people involved with the family, their relationships and what the areas of concern are. I emphasize to the parents that this initial separate session will be their only opportunity to talk about the past, as all joint sessions will focus on the present and the future only. Nothing can be done to go back and change the past and it is highly unlikely that both parents will ever agree about who was at fault in any given situation. At this point, the therapist needs to start looking at the issues and potential areas of intervention. As this is an individual session, pointers/suggestions/advice can be given to the parent to try to give him or her strategies for approaching the other parent differently with a greater chance of success.

...it is highly unlikely that both parents will ever agree about who was at fault in any given situation.

If the parent appears strongly caught up in the emotion surrounding the divorce, individual counselling may also be suggested and a referral may be made to another therapist or the client can be directed to a referral service, such as the local psychological association. This individual therapist would be entirely outside of the Family Restructuring Therapy process and no contact would take place between the parent's therapist and the person conducting Family Restructuring Therapy. To do so would be another form of one-sided communication that is not allowed in this process. As a cautionary note, it is important that referrals be made to therapists who recognize parents need to put the needs of their children first and to not make the parents into lifelong hedonistic victims. A negative example occurred when a therapist stated that a parent had been so traumatized in her marriage that she should never have to even hear the other parent's name spoken aloud again as long as she lived. Not a practical thought, when the two parents shared 5 children between the ages of 4 and 12.

In the first session I am quite blunt with the parents telling them, "I'm sure you've seen the stereotype of the psychologist who asks you how you feel. To me, it's not your feelings that are important; rather, it is how you behave, as my primary concern in this process is the well-being of your children." Other partners in my practice make a similar statement in a much gentler way, which is equally effective. **However, the primary emphasis is**

on the parents acting in an appropriate manner to make life better for the children, and on the expectation of the parents that they will control their emotions and place their children's needs first.

Finally, I ask the parents to describe what the major issues are that need to be addressed, what has been tried to address these problems in the past and what they could do differently in the future to more successfully deal with the problem. The emphasis is on what the parents can do in the future and it is clearly pointed out to them that they are "100% in charge of 50% of the parenting relationship and 0% in charge of the other 50%." All we can focus on is what they can do. It is pointed out that to rely on the other parent to change is giving the other parent control over the parenting relationship and even the happiness of the other parent.

In the individual session, I spend a significant amount of time describing the negative effects of conflict in divorce on their children and the potential negative outcomes that could take place. Parents are informed that high-conflict divorce has been related to emotional problems, behavioural problems, academic/learning problems, depression and anxiety, substance abuse, antisocial behaviour, high school dropout, suicide/self harm, not attending postsecondary, poor relationships as an adult, and even lower career attainment for children living in a high-conflict divorce. I view this as my "ghost of Christmas future" process, as I have worked with children in one role or another (instructor, teacher, school counsellor, psychologist) since 1974 and my sole reason for doing Family Restructuring Therapy is to prevent the damage I have observed in children and teens over many years. **As Mr. Justice Harvey Brownstone (2009) stated, the parents need to place their love of the children above their dislike, or hate, or each other.**

Finally, the parent is told that in the next (joint) session I will be asking each of them to bring a list of issues that need to be addressed and that I want these issues described in as few words as possible without placing blame. For example, rather than saying, "I want the other parent to have the children phone me when they're supposed to", it should be worded as, "I would like to come up with effective telephone communication between the children and the parents", or even more briefly put, "telephone communication".

The first parent to attend the initial appointment is told that at the end of the second parent's appointment he or she will be phoned so that a mutually agreeable time can be set for the first joint appointment. When the second parent comes in, I contact the first parent by phone (not on speaker) and arrange a suitable meeting time for the first joint appointment. At this stage, occasionally one or both parents state that it is simply impossible to meet during office hours or over the next few months, at which point they are both told that their lawyers and/or the court will be contacted of the impasse. While some may be willing to work evenings and weekends, I do not as part of my own self care. To make an analogy, if you want an appointment for most medical/dental or other specialists, you are generally told when the appointment is and given little choice if it fits your schedule or not. The Family Restructuring Therapy is a specialized service provided by extensively trained and experienced therapists. You can view parents coming to you as having "cancer of the relationship" and they need to make getting healthy a priority in their lives.

C. The First Joint Session

While it may seem somewhat redundant, the first joint session begins in a similar manner to the first individual sessions. The purpose here is to reaffirm the process with both parents present and to emphasize the rules for parental behaviour and the need to keep a future-only focus. Examples can be given to re-word issues such as:

"You let the children play video games that are inappropriate" too. "I would like it if we could get a strategy to decide which video games our children can and cannot play."

For a large portion of the first joint session, neither parent is allowed to talk and the therapist needs to be a good judge of body language and nonverbal communication to see how the parents are reacting to what is being said to them. I also start by telling them that neither parent is allowed to take notes during the session, and that if any agreements are reached I will write them down and give both of them copies. It is emphasized that such notes, while not legally binding, are important in that it is an agreement they have reached. Parents are always told that when they come close to making a decision, they have 3 options: to agree, to disagree, or to say they need to take time to think about it and will report back next session. However, it is emphasized that if both parents agree to any new strategy, neither one of them can unilaterally go back on an agreement outside of the session and that changes can only be made during sessions. A significant amount of time is also spent emphasizing the potential damage to children when their parents are in high-conflict with one another. If common issues/concerns about any of the children have been raised by both parents, at times I explain the theoretical damage that could take place given what is actually going on, based on their reports of the children.

Behavioural expectations of the parent's include:

- Parents are instructed that unless a situation appears life threatening, no calls can be made to police or child protective services and that any concerns will be reported to their therapist.

- If destructive communication is taking place between the parents, this communication is put on hold and the therapist directs the communication process.
- When parents are instructed to resume direct communication they will follow clearly established rules.
- Parents are taught to utilise effective communication skills.
- Parents are reminded that they cannot demand or direct the other parent.
- Parents are educated regarding parenting and child development issues.
- Clear boundaries are established. Parents are advised that as long as the child is not experiencing a difficulty, each parent is allowed to do what they believe is best.
- If a significant problem with the child does arise, the parents are assisted in developing a joint plan to address the problem.
- If the parents start to verbally fight they will be asked to stop. If they start arguing again, they will be asked to leave that session and the session (not the process) is terminated.

The first joint session also describes common reactions of children of divorce, such as the tendency of the children to tell the parents what they want to hear rather than the truth. The parents are told how important it is for the child to have as many healthy, appropriate parents in their lives as possible and that qualifiers such as step, half or ex- are irrelevant from a child's perspective. Children have brothers and sisters, grandparents and parents. Further distinctions are not required.

The parents are told they can refer to each other as "dad" or "mom" or by their first names, but they need to refer to one another with respect. I tell them to quit using the word "ex" with respect to one another, as it appears degrading and that neither of them has the right to refer to themselves as a single parent, because there are, in fact, two parents for their children. I often speak of the "hit by a bus" theory, in that if one parent successfully turned the children against the other parent and then something tragic happens to them, their children are left as orphans in the world rather than having another parent to go to.

> ... if they both want to be in charge
> of the process, they don't need to
> come see me.

It is finally the parents turn to speak and it is important to quickly and decisively stop them from saying anything inappropriate, and if they do I use it as a teaching opportunity to show them how it could be better worded. The first task is for each parent to describe the list of topics each would like to raise during therapy. I point to the bookcase in my office and tell them that what I want them to list are like titles in a book describing topics such as "schedule, extracurricular, bedtime routine, etc." without providing any details and definitely without taking any shots at the other person. I gently spin a pen on the coffee table and whoever it points to is the first to give a list. The other parent is told to focus on waiting to recite their list rather than reacting to the list given by the first parent. The lists are then obtained from each parent, with the therapist interjecting appropriate wording and stopping inappropriate comments and complementing positive communication. The therapist continually works with the parents to change their language from identifying problems to offering solutions.

As the process is run by the therapist, I then arrange the list in the order I want to address topics, rather than in the order either parent might want. Almost inevitably "communication" is on both lists and is frequently the best topic to start with. While the therapist can ask at each session if there are any time-sensitive or urgent topics to address, keep two things in mind: first, a parent continually coming with one crisis or another is actually sabotaging the process and taking charge of what is addressed. I often tell parents that if they both want to be in charge of the process, they don't need to come see me. They can continue fighting in their previously unsuccessful manner without paying for the cost of a psychologist. Second, as is taught in areas such as solution-focused/brief therapy, people in dysfunction keep trying their best to resolve the problems. Unfortunately, if left to their own devices, they will likely try the same thing repeatedly with equally unsuccessful results. A significant contribution from the therapist is to itemize and prioritize topics and to keep parents appropriately on one topic from start to finish before going on to another. Typical arguments between high-conflict individuals are anything but linear. One parent will start with topic 1, the other parent will switch to topic 2 and 3, with the first parent returning to topic 1 and adding topic 4. The other parent will then disagree with topic 4 and give a rapid-fire list of topics 5, 6, 7 and 8 before the first parent says, "See! There's just no talking to that person". The typical pattern of arguments can be broken, with the therapist selecting the topics and selecting when to switch topics.

D. Communication

As stated, the first topic to address is usually the communication style between parents. If you think of a child playing with building blocks in an unsophisticated manner, the child often tries to make a tower by placing one stack of blocks next to another and next to another, until at some point the whole tower falls over looking like a banana peeling itself. To extend the metaphor, it is necessary to take parent's communication back to a very simple, and accountable, level. It is rare to find parents that do not have access to email, so the first agreement we generally reach is that, except in emergencies, the parents will communicate by email only; however, they must follow a very strict set of rules:

Rules for E-Mail Communication
- Maximum one email per day from either parent.
- Maximum one issue per email.
- Maximum 40 words per email.
- Parent must respond to email (yes, no, I don't know, let's leave this for counselling) within 24 hours but cannot respond within 3 hours (to give time to think/cool down before responding).
- Only topics pertaining directly to the child may be addressed.
- Emails must be future-focused and polite.
- Emails are to be copied to the therapist. (This builds in a degree of accountability.)
- In emergency situations that immediately affect the child and cannot wait, the 3-hour rule or one email per day rule does not apply.
- In extreme medical emergencies for the child, telephone contact will occur as soon as possible.

After the email rules are agreed upon, make sure each parent has the other parent's email address and that both parents have your email address. I tend to look at the first few quite closely, and, especially if both parents are not following the rules, send a reply to both of them reminding them of what they agreed to, so they stay on topic. Other times, it can be helpful to send a brief email to both parents with positive reinforcement for appropriate interactions.

Usually by this point there is no time to raise other issues, so subsequent appointments are booked. If an agreement on email has been reached, each parent is given a copy of the agreement page. An agreement sheet is very simple and to the point. The one I use looks like this:

Topic:_____

Decision: _____

_____

_____

Date: _____

Parent Signatures: _____

_____

I typically have a large stack of these blank sheets in my office. In the case of communication, the decision could be as simple as, "both parents agree to communicate by email only, except in emergencies and to follow the attached email rules." I also have the email rules on my office computer that can be easily modified for each family to include email addresses or any changes required.

E. Developing a Parenting Plan

There are multiple examples of parenting plans to be found. The problem with most of them is that they are theoretical and non-specific. An important aspect of dealing with high-conflict parents is making all decisions as clear as possible with nothing left open for interpretation. **Even high-conflict parents can function well with strict guidelines, careful preplanning and predictability. Where they tend to fall off the rails is with any parenting issue that requires spontaneous decision-making.** The parenting plan format I have developed first looks at common important issues such as the parenting schedule and how to make exceptions to the schedule and exchanges. It is followed by a list of potential topics for the parenting plan. Some, or many, of these topics would not apply at all to the parents of a newborn, while others would be irrelevant for the parents of a 16-year-old. The way I make use of it is to have each parent identify the parenting issues they want to have input on. Then we go through all of them and identify topics where we need to come up with guidelines and procedures for parenting. With some parents, they race through the list of parenting issues, which can also reinforce that they are doing some things well as parents. With other parents, the process can be painstakingly slow.

Guiding values for the development of parenting plans include:

- Appropriate parents are primary caregivers.
- Stability of placement is considered in the context of developmental needs.
- A harmonious parenting relationship is more important than any extracurricular activity the child could be enrolled in.

- The needs of the older child for peer contact and changing parent/child relationship must be considered.
- School age children need multiple parenting plans: school year, summer vacation, winter vacation, and spring break.
- Regardless of the schedule, the children will be with their mother on her birthday and Mother's Day and with father on his birthday and Father's Day.
- Children can benefit from one-on-one time with each parent.
- Parents must cooperate to provide as many opportunities for their child as possible.
- Clear definitions of terms are required, e.g. the weekend begins when child leaves school for the last time before Saturday and ends when the child enters school for the first time after Sunday.

Keep in mind that the therapist is doing parallel processes: working on the practical restructuring of parental processes, while also working with the parents on communication and problem solving. The therapist also has a gatekeeper role of keeping the parents on topic on parenting issues, while setting strict boundaries regarding personal issues that should no longer be discussed. The guidebook I use with parents in developing their plan is found in Appendix 1 at the back of this book.

F. Subsequent Joint Sessions

In subsequent sessions it is important for the therapist to keep referring back to the list of issues, to maintain consistency and direction. I generally start each session by first asking if there are any time-sensitive issues that need to be addressed. Caution is needed to minimize the tendency of parents to continually chase crises, as opposed to methodically addressing issues one by one. Often, one of the problems for the family prior to counselling was that everything was a crisis. While this is not functional behaviour, it is one way that the parents can elicit a strong emotional response from one another and they can delay moving forward and healing from grief.

The second thing I do in each subsequent session is address any emails that have been monitored since the previous session. Especially important is to comment whether the rules are being followed or not, and to actively coach both participants as to how they could communicate better with one another.

> Caution is needed to minimize the tendency of parents to continually chase crises...

Sessions need to be strictly controlled and agreements need to be documented. Often, important issues to address include how to problem-solve, how to make exceptions to the schedule, how out-of-country travel should be handled and how extracurricular activities should be selected. Following are some guidelines that can be helpful for these areas:

F.1. Problem-Solving

The first step in problem-solving is to break a given problem into as many specific problems as possible. Often, the reason families are unsuccessful in addressing problems is that they are actually addressing multiple problems at once, without both parents having a clear focus on what must be decided. Once the problem is broken down into as many possible "sub-problems" as possible, the therapist can prioritize and guide the parents through the following process, dealing with one problem at a time:

- **Identify and define the problem.** Both parents need to have a clear understanding of what the problem actually is, so that they are actually working on the same issue.

- **List what you know/don't know.** Many misunderstandings come from incomplete information or mistaken assumptions. It's kind of like putting together a puzzle without checking if you have all the pieces. Often in the process of listing what is known and what is not known the solution emerges on its own.

- **Get further information.** It is often necessary to gather additional information before an informed decision can be made. This could include what the boundaries are for schools the children may want to go to and whether they allowed to go to a school outside of their boundary; what it takes to obtain a passport or travel out of the country; or if the child requires braces or allergy testing. Again, rather than the parents just speculating, directing the parents to decide what information is necessary and who will obtain it can go a long way toward deciding an issue. This is also why it is important for the children to only have one physician, one dentist, etc., so that information or advice will come from someone who has some knowledge of the child.

- **Look at all the options.** This is the "brainstorming" portion of problem solving. Here the therapist can also introduce additional options, as parents in conflict are both so entrenched with their own views of the solution, they do not have awareness of all the different possibilities. A creative, experienced therapist can be of great benefit to the parents at this stage.

- **Narrow down to the best option.** Now that all of the options and information is available, the parents can be guided to narrowing down the list based on the needs of their child and the reality of the situation. For example, while the parents may want their children to attend an exclusive private school on the other side of town, it is not a practical option if both parents lack the ability to pay for the school fees or if the children would have to take public transportation, transferring three times and spending two hours each direction.

- **Select and implement the option.** Here the focus must be kept on what is good for the child and what is practical. A guiding principle is that if changes are to be made there should be a clearly demonstrated benefit for the child. While the consistency and stability of an established routine should be viewed as important, divorced families are encouraged to come up with new routines that will be of benefit to the children. I often tell parents that if they cannot see themselves having a joint birthday party or Christmas day celebration with the children, perhaps they could work towards a small dinner involving only the 2 parents and the children in the week preceding such events.

- **Evaluate the solution at a later time.** Setting a time to evaluate the solution (such as in 3 weeks, 6 months or one year) keeps the parents committed to implementing the solution until the evaluation time, rather than superficially trying to implement the agreed upon change, only to abandon it because "it didn't work". Parents need to be told that a new discipline program for the children may take six months or more of consistent implementation to show benefit, or that the children may not know whether they truly like a new activity until they have attended it at least six times.

F.2 Exceptions to the Schedule

This is another common area of conflict between parents. It is inappropriate to involve a child in a decision regarding an exception to the schedule, before it is discussed with the other Parent, whether due to honest motives or dishonest motives (such as trying to bribe the child away from the other parent during the other parent's time). Asking the children if they want to go skiing the following weekend if the other parent will allow it, is often a no-win situation. The parent who is being asked to give up the children can open the door to multiple exceptions and being pushed around, or risks being viewed as the mean parent who does not allow the child to have fun.

Some guidelines for exceptions to the schedule are:
- If an opportunity for the child comes up on the other parent's parenting time:
- Before the child is made aware of the opportunity, the parent wishing the change contacts the other parent without the child's knowledge.
- If the change is allowed, the child is informed.
- If the change is denied, the child never knows of the missed opportunity.

The other component to discuss with the parents is to point out that the children are only young for a certain number of years and it is the parent's job to provide them with as many exciting and stimulating opportunities as possible. I often point out that conflict in families arises over three basic areas: time, money and energy. The one area hardest hit for most parents after divorce is money, as the family now requires two households rather than one. It is even more important that the parents work together, so that potential missed opportunities are minimized for the children. I generally tell parents that from birth through grade 6, they will be the center of the children's universe. Starting as early as grade 7, if the children are developing socially as they should, the parents are still important, but their most frequent roles become cook, chauffeur and personal shopper.

F.3 Out- of-Country Travel

Similar to exceptions to the schedule, a clear process for out of country travel makes life much easier for planning vacations. Sometimes this travel will involve a change in parenting time, other times it simply involves a notarized letter to clear customs. I often encourage parents who are working reasonably well together and who are in the process of obtaining their final divorce judgment, to have it put into the court order that either parent is allowed to take the children out of the country for travel. This can save significant time and money over the years, in contrast to continually obtaining notarized letters. Some parents develop a form letter with specifics such as dates and contact information to be filled in each time as necessary. The goal is to make the process as simple as possible to minimize opportunity for disagreement or misunderstanding.

Guidelines that can be implemented are:

- Traveling parent informs the other parent of desire and provides as many details as possible.
- If permission is granted, a letter of permission is provided.
- Upon receipt of the letter of permission, travel arrangements are made and a copy of the complete itinerary (flights, hotels, dates, contact numbers) is provided to the non-traveling parent.

The parents need to realize where the boundaries are in situations such as travel. The non-traveling parent should always know where their children will be sleeping each night, how to reach the children in an emergency and travel details. For example, if the children are going to Japan Disneyland, flight information and hotel information needs to be provided, but the non-traveling parent has no business dictating what the children eat for breakfast or which rides they go on at the amusement park.

F.4 Extracurricular Activity

While extracurricular activity is a wonderful enhancement for the physical, intellectual, emotional and social development of children, no one activity is more important than the parent-child relationship. Steps to ensure that extracurricular activities are benefits, not detriments, to the children include:

- Need to be agreed upon before registration takes place.
- Once agreed upon, the activity is not the parent's activity but the child's. Both parents are responsible to ensure attendance and both parents are able to attend (when appropriate) to watch the child.

- Parents are expected to work cooperatively to ensure attendance.
- In some cases, one parent will drive all the time to a certain activity as long as both parents agree upon this in advance.
- If one parent is taking the child to and from a specific activity and the other parent attends, it is a good practice to ensure that the parent transporting the child has the child speak to the other parent before leaving with an opportunity to say goodbye. This way the child does not feel torn between her parents and the activity has a greater opportunity to be enjoyable.

Other Information on Subsequent Joint Sessions

It is always the goal of therapy for therapists to work themselves out of a job. As parents progress, I encourage them to switch from coming every week to coming every second week. I encourage them to address issues as they arise through email, by telephone (only as progress is being made and as long as the children are not present at either end) or even meeting at a coffee shop and acting as if it was a therapy session. The parents are also told that, no matter what the issue is, they always have the option to agree, disagree, offer an alternative or modification, or tell the other parent that he or she would like to discuss the issue in the next therapy session.

It is almost a magical moment in the therapy office when the parents switch from "me-me-me" and "I-I-I" to jointly discussing what needs to be done for their child. The parents become engaged with one another, talk about what the child needs rather than blaming the other parent, and the atmosphere is far less charged emotionally. Compliments and compromises are more often seen. At this point, due to my somewhat blunt style, after letting the parents successfully communicate for a while I will say something like "Okay, hold it a minute. Who are you and what did you do with the other parents. What I see in front of me are two fantastic parents who are focusing on the needs of the child and working together as a family. Where did this come from and what can be done to keep it going?" I will even go as far, if appropriate, as having each parent give the other parent feedback about how much he or she enjoys being able to enter into such positive parenting conversations.

> It is always the goal of therapy
> for therapists to work themselves
> out of a job.

G. Report Writing

At different times in the process of Family Restructuring Therapy, a report is produced which either goes to the lawyers for the parents or directly to the Court. Report writing takes on four different forms, depending on whether Family Restructuring Therapy was successful or unsuccessful.

G.1 Successful Family

For the successful family, the report can be as simple as, "Kelly Weston and Pat Smith have now completed Family Restructuring Therapy. They have resolved all issues pertaining to parenting time, extracurricular activities, vacation schedules and schools for the children and have shown a significant improvement in their communication and problem solving ability. At this point no further sessions are planned, although the parents are free to return if issues arise that they need assistance with. Rather than requiring a retainer for such sessions, the parents will pay as sessions are needed. It has been a pleasure working with this family and it is thought that the outlook for the well-being of both Kim and Jordan is positive."

I enjoy sending such letters and I believe that lawyers and the Court also enjoy seeing that there are some high-conflict families that do succeed.

G.2 Interim Report - Further Sessions Required

Interim reports requiring further sessions are best kept brief. It should list the dates of sessions so far, it can include copies of agreements made to that point and a non-descriptive list of outstanding issues that still need to be worked on. Statements such as, "one parent appears more inappropriate", "another has difficulty with punctuality" or any other description of behaviour, which could be interpreted as positive or negative, may give the impression that one parent is "better" than the other and lead to the process being prematurely terminated. It is no different than when a therapist needs to testify in court regarding a counselling client. Such testimony can negatively impact the therapist-client relationship and make it difficult to continue with counselling.

G.3 Issues to be Addressed by the Court

At times, the parents will reach a deadlock and the matter needs to be referred back to the court for a decision. Typically the letter would include the sessions to date, the agreements made, the outstanding issue(s), and what is needed from the court.

Unfortunately, the most frequent letter states, "On a variety of topics the parents keep returning to their disagreement over how financial matters will be settled and state they are not able to make a decision until they are aware of their financial status. As Family Restructuring Therapy does not include addressing financial concerns, and because such concerns are preventing progress in this process, this process has now been placed on hold. It is strongly recommended that all financial issues be dealt with by the lawyers/court immediately so that this process can resume. It is unfortunate that the parents view money as being more important than their children." I often put in this last sentence, especially if both parents are letting money get in the way of parenting decisions. However, I understand that many therapists would not be comfortable being this forceful. For me, this is something the parents have already heard, as I tell them that placing money before their children is inexcusable.

G.4 Unsuccessful Family Restructuring Therapy

Unfortunately, there is not a happy ending to every story. Keep in mind that we are starting with a skewed population of high-conflict individuals who often have a history of court battles and unsuccessful mental health interventions. When parents do not make sufficient progress to protect the children from conflict, a more structured court intervention, such as parallel parenting, is required. In other cases, the court may have to order sole custody with limited contact towards a continually inappropriate parent. However, that would be the decision of the court or the recommendation of an assessor.

Unfortunately, there is not a happy
ending to every story.

Even when the process seems unsuccessful, experience has shown that it may alter some aspects of communication which result in less exposure to conflict for the children. Hopefully, in other cases the parents are just not yet ready to hear the message, but it may "sink in" over time. Sometimes it just doesn't work and the parents continue to resist any attempt at changing their behaviours.

For the unsuccessful family, the report will include the following components:

- Referral goals and referral source - similar to what was on the retainer agreement.
- Dates of sessions, who attended, who missed appointments.
- Agreements made to date - here I will copy out what was written down on the individual sheets and state what date they were made on.
- Outstanding issues that have not been resolved - including, if possible, each parent's position on those issues and where the deadlocks may exist.
- Parental behaviour during sessions - keep in mind this is just a narrative not evaluative; only objectively describe the behaviour without interpreting it.
- Recommendation for further services - which could include stating that perhaps an open custody assessment, addressing this in court, or some other service could assist the family with their difficulties.

CHAPTER 7

Working with Parents in a
Therapeutic Team Approach

Where the conflict between parents is extreme or where there is a significant history of violence (or allegation of violence), it is best to have a team approach in working with the parents. With this approach, one therapist works with one parent, another therapist works with the other, and joint sessions involve both therapists. An advantage of this approach is that individual parent-therapist sessions can take place outside of the joint session, to help each parent work on their individual issues related to parenting and to provide individual coaching.

In extreme high-conflict families, there are two clear advantages of utilizing a therapeutic team, where each parent has their own therapist. First, it allows each therapist to give much more immediate feedback during joint sessions or in individual sessions, creating an environment where clear expectations for "doing things differently" exists. In single therapist sessions, while it is important to shut down inappropriate behaviour, the therapist needs to be careful to have a balanced approach to addressing negatives in the parents. I often wait until both parents have shown a similar negative attitude or belief before addressing it. Otherwise, the risk is that one parent feels singled out and therefore wants to withdraw from the process, because you are "not being fair". The second advantage of having two therapists is that there is great potential for teaching and modeling. At times, the therapists can take over the conversation and demonstrate healthy communication styles. It is important to have experienced therapists working with Family Restructuring Therapy, so that both therapists do not inadvertently identify with their clients and simply mirror the dysfunctional communication pattern. To be honest, there is also a third advantage to working with the therapeutic team. Working with high-conflict parents can be very trying and it is definitely a bonus to have another individual with whom to brainstorm, consult and commiserate.

> ...advantage of having two therapists is that there is great potential for teaching and modeling.

The process begins with each parent having an individual session. This first session has two components: orientation and evaluating the strengths and weaknesses of the parent. This is virtually the same as first sessions with single therapist interventions, except you are also looking at ways you will be able to work with the individual parent. If there is a custody assessment that has been completed, you can review the summary and recommendations with the client to focus on the things they need to do. This can begin to build accountability:

Introduction
  1. Review the court order and/or retainer agreement
  2. Inform the parent of the goals of the process.

3. Review the general strategy regarding the series of appointments.

4. Remind the parent of the limits of confidentiality.

5. Ask the parent to review the relevant history, identify parenting/access issues to be addressed.

6. Remind the parent that the focus of the process is to move forward from this point.

7. Look for: parent's relationship with the child, parent's strengths, needs, fears, resistance to moving forward, hopes for the future, distortion in beliefs and perceptions.

While you are not doing a formal assessment of the parent, the next step is for you to identify the strengths and liabilities of the parent you are working with, including the following points:

1. Identify the primary needs of the individual parent, i.e. to be a good parent, to retaliate for perceived or real hurts, to ensure the child's safety while with the other parent, etc.

2. Identify the parent's strengths.

3. Separate the parent's needs and experience from the child's needs and experience.

4. Educate the parent about the value of supporting and strengthening the child's relationship with the other parent.

5. Utilize the parent's strengths to encourage personal leadership and responsibility for behaviour during the process of separation and divorce.

6. Address distortions in beliefs and perceptions.

7. Address parenting skills, communication skills, problem-solving skills, and crisis management skills as required.

8. Identify and address any overt or covert attempts to undermine the process.

9. Help the parent look at alternative (and hopefully positive) reasons for the behaviours of the other parent.

During your work with the parent, it is important to reinforce positive behaviours and changes made by the parent.

1. Teach, model and coach positive behavioural change.

2. Reinforce constructive behavioural change.

3. Identify the benefits to the child.

4. Confront conscious or unconscious efforts to undermine the child's well-being.

The first joint session and subsequent sessions generally follow the same format as listed previously for single therapist interventions. However, the key difference is the tight control each therapist has on the parent that therapist is working with, to keep him from saying inappropriate things and to shut him down immediately should he lapse into negative communication patterns. The focus of communication is also a bit different in the two therapist model: rather than each parent telling a single therapist what items to put on the agenda, each parent tells his or her own therapist in front of the others what he or she would like to address, with the individual therapist actively coaching the client how to frame topics in a simple, future-focused and non-confrontational fashion. Whether you are using a single or double therapist model, the parents are not allowed to directly address each other until they have demonstrated appropriate and respectful communication with the therapist. In the next step, the two therapists typically will have a discussion as to what they want to address first, second, third, etc. and to build the agenda accordingly. As always, the focus is on the needs of the child, not the needs of the parent, and with parents, not children, responsible for making major family decisions. When working with the parents jointly for the first session, I would again go over all of the potential damage parental conflict can do to the children.

In this model it is also easier to take detailed notes. When one parent is talking and being coached by his or her therapist, the other therapist has more freedom to write down what is being said. Remember that generally these are families in extreme conflict and, even if they are not successful in counselling, a detailed description of the sessions can assist the court if things do not work out.

All subsequent sessions start with the therapists asking their own clients how they (not how the other person) followed through on previous agreements. The therapists then consult, in front of the clients, as to what topic to cover next and they work through the agenda one topic at a time.

An important point is that both therapists are equally diligent at shutting down their own clients. It comes across as inappropriate for the therapist of one parent to stop the other parent, if the parent is behaving inappropriately.

Working with the Children

The different reasons for working with children in Family Restructuring Therapy include:

- To provide ongoing support for children in a difficult situation and to help them cope the best they can. In this case, little or no feedback is provided to the parents.

- To have a third party obtain their true opinions on a variety of issues, as children in high-conflict divorce quite often tell each parent what they want to hear, at times giving opposing information to each parent. In this case, the parent's therapist can consult with the children's therapist (to check out such situations).

- To work with angry or alienated children, to help them reconnect with the "rejected" parent. This point will be addressed in the next chapter.

This work can only be done by therapists who are trained and experienced in working with children and teens.

Like any form of counselling, the first session must start with describing the process to the child in a manner that is age-appropriate and discussing issues of confidentiality. Assuring confidentiality for any issues that do not fall under the category of mandatory reporting (abuse, life or death) is often important in establishing rapport. The children must be clearly informed whether information will be shared with their parents or not, whether information could be subpoenaed by the court, and whether they would have input in advance as to what would be shared. Generally, children are willing for their parents to become aware of how the divorce and their parents' behaviour have affected them.

In the first session or two with children, the therapist tries to formulate what the issues are from the child's perspective.

Topics covered include:

1. Who all the people are in the child's family: parents, siblings, new partners for their parents, stepsiblings, extended family and other relevant individuals. In pre-teen, school age children, this can start with the child creating and describing a family drawing.

2. When the separation took place, what the living arrangements have been like from then and up to the current time. Find out what works about the arrangements and what are the difficult parts.

3. What schools the child has attended.

4. The child's perception of the divorce, including both positive factors (e.g. less fighting) and the negative factors.

5. Relationships among family members and other significant individuals.

6. What the parents say to the child about the divorce and about the other parent.

7. What comments siblings and other family members make to the child regarding other family members or parents.

8. What changes the child feels need to be made, to make his or her life easier, and what message the child would like to pass on to the parents, if they had the opportunity to sit them both down and talk to them.

9. An examination of the psychological/behavioural functioning of the child that can include such factors as depression, anxiety, somatization, substance abuse, suicidal thoughts, thoughts of running away, aggression, school difficulty as well as positive factors such as support systems and extracurricular activities.

10. Who the child identifies as supports.

11. What the child would like to get out of attending counselling (goals).

In the first sessions, it is important to allow the child to freely express his thoughts and feelings without being challenged. In later interviews, if the therapist has been made aware of specific concerns in the case, the therapist, questioning gently, probes some of the more contentious issues that exist within the divorce.

During the first interviews, the therapist is trying to determine what the child's perception of family issues and problems is; if what the child is saying matches her age and developmental level; or, if she appears to be parroting what she may have been told directly or heard indirectly from adults. An important task here is to look for the presence of genuine, age appropriate and developmental level concerns that are expressed in reasonable detail. Often, children who have taken sides, or who have been encouraged to take sides, will repeat a "mantra" of one or two trivial issues again and again as if not getting a pony ride for their eighth birthday explains all the problems they have with a parent six years later.

Generally, children are willing
for their parents to become aware
of how the divorce and their parents'
behaviour have affected them.

It is helpful to have the parents alternate bringing the child to counselling. You are then able to observe the child, even briefly at drop off and pick up, in a natural setting. This can provide important non-verbal information about relationships and even parenting styles.

It is important in working with the child that you are able to provide age-appropriate coping strategies, without making the child feel responsible for the family. One of the first things I often do is talk about grief and loss as it is related to divorce. By telling serious, or funny, stories about how other children have reacted to a family break-up, it allows the children to talk more openly about their experiences. More importantly, it helps them recognize that they are normal. I will ask them outright if they have started telling parents things that are not true, just to make them happy. The majority of times the answer is yes.

We generally spend a lot of time talking about the different roles within the family. For example, what a parent is responsible for and what a child is responsible for. With older children, I point out that there is no role in life more important than being a parent and that it makes parents feel good to be able to help their children, even if the problem the children are experiencing is a parent or the divorce. We talk about ways the children have tried to address concerns, and see if there are alternatives that could be tried for the children to communicate more effectively.

I give the children permission to quote me to their parents, most commonly, "Steve said that I am allowed to love both my parents and if people say bad things about either parent I should be allowed to walk away so I don't have to hear it." Before recommending this, you need to have a clear understanding of the family dynamics and a strong belief that such a statement would not make things worse for the child.

Subsequent sessions examine the stresses the children are under and provide an opportunity to help them in developing coping skills or in learning how to solicit support from their parents. The children can be helped to move in a positive direction, by having discussions of what it will be like when all the problems with one or both parents have been successfully resolved. Those of you experienced in solution-focused/brief therapy may recognize many parallels here, such as trying to change the family system by having the child do something different, as long as it is an appropriate task for a child and that it does not "parentify" them; and asking the "miracle question" of what things will look like when everything is better.

When working with the child and the parent of different genders—for example a daughter and a father— it can be helpful to tell the child the need to give the parent information about being a girl (or boy), as they are continually changing as they grow up. It's emphasized that the children have important information to tell the parents, but it is not up to them to solve adult problems.

If there is more than one child involved, I tend to recommend separate therapists. I try to coordinate it so that the children's appointments are all at the same time and they do not have to spend extended time in the waiting room. On occasion, I have reluctantly worked with two children in the family, but I never have them in the same session or discuss with one child what the other has said. Despite this, it can be helpful on rare occasions to have siblings together for a brief time to observe the dynamics between them. Dynamics can also be observed between siblings or parents and children in the waiting room.

It is especially important to have separate therapists when the children involved have taken different "sides" in the dispute.

When it comes time for providing feedback to the parents, there are different ways that this can be done.

First, unsolicited feedback can be given to the parents. For example, I could ask a child if he wanted to write a letter to his parents to let them know how things are affecting him and what improvements (in parental behaviour, not in living arrangements) could be made. This is most often done when the child describes both parents as behaving equally badly. Sometimes, with bright and articulate children, the first version of the letter is perfect and it can be given to the parent's therapist to discuss with the parents. Other times, revision is needed to separate out appropriate issues from inappropriate issues for the child's input, and how to word the letter in such a way that it has the best chance of success. I pass these letters on to the parents through their therapists. I have also gone into a parent's individual session to provide the information from the child and to give my concerns about what the parental behaviour is doing to the child and how it will impact the child's future. In these cases I tend to give my best "Ghost of Christmas Future" impression.

> "Tell my parents that they're the adults and I'm the kid and I will be fine with whatever they decide on as long as they quit fighting about it."

Second, solicited feedback can be requested by the parent's therapist. For example, there was a case where a child had a choice of going to a grandparent's home for lunch or staying at school and taking part in intramurals. Apparently, the child had told one parent (the one related to the grandparent) that the preference would be to visit the grandparents for lunch, while the child also told the other parent the child would rather stay at school for intramurals. The question asked of the child was simply, "Tell me what kind of things you like to do during your lunch hour at school." Interestingly, the child responded with a desire to go to the grandparents house for lunch two days a week when there was "nothing much going on at school," to take part in intramurals on Tuesday and Thursday, and to be at school Friday for lunch "just to hang out with friends." The child then agreed that this information could be passed on to the parents. In another case, I was working with the parents and one of my partners, Bonnie, was working with the child. Bonnie asked the child, "Did you tell your mom that you wanted to live full-time with her?" The child replied, "Yes." She then asked, "Did you tell your dad that you wanted to live full-time with him?" The child also replied, "Yes." The child was asked how that could occur and after looking puzzled for a few moments replied, "Maybe they could get married again." Just because a child tells you something, doesn't mean it is possible or practical, but it does show how the child views a perfect world. In all cases, the child is asked for permission to pass on information to the parents.

A final example is one of my favourites. I was working with a 13-year-old boy and the parents wanted to know his thoughts on the issues, solutions and schedule. I had started by telling him I would only report what he allowed me to. In the first session he went on and on describing at length what was wrong and how to fix it. In the second session he walked in and said, "Steve, did you really mean it when you said you're only going to tell my parents what I want them to know?" I replied that I had meant it and he stated, "Write this down. Tell my parents that they're the adults and I'm the kid and I will be fine with whatever they decide on as long as they quit fighting about it."

It took a lot restraint on my part to not stand up and cheer such an appropriate and insightful response.

As the child's therapist, it takes some measure of skill to keep the parents from being able to corner you through phone calls, email or while bringing the child to an appointment. In such cases, it is important to repeat the same thing over and over again: "My job is to work with your child. While I am sure what you have to say is important, it needs to be discussed by both parents and their therapist, and your therapist will inform me of anything I need to know."

Finally, when parents are engaged in a high-conflict dispute, they are often emotionally unavailable for the child. It is important that the child has at least one trusted adult to talk to and at times you become that person. When this is the case, another therapeutic task is to help identify, if possible, other adults the child can turn to for support (aunts/uncles, grandparents, trusted neighbours, teachers, etc.).

CHAPTER 9

Working with Families When the Children Have Rejected a Parent

The last application of Family Restructuring Therapy is parent-child reunification. To simplify describing this process, the parents will be called the "preferred parent" and the "rejected parent." All the same skills described in working with parents and children already discussed are required for doing this process. The process can be done with one therapist, with two therapists (one for the child and one for the parents) or in extreme cases with three therapists (one for the child and one for each parent). As with the other processes, an initial retainer letter is essential to cover what can and cannot be addressed, that it is an open process and what the process looks like.

The goal of the sessions is to rebuild damaged parent-child relationships while assuring the safety of the child. It is important to give the child age-appropriate control of the speed of the process while not making the process itself optional. **The therapist does not want to appear aligned with either parent and the ultimate goal is for the child to have a positive relationship with both parents.** While the parents often come to this process with a simple "good versus evil" theme, the reality is that both parents need to be meaningfully involved in the child's life for healthy development.

The steps of parent-child reunification therapy (after the retainer letter has been provided) are:

1. Meeting with the Preferred Parent

    The first step is to meet with the parent with whom the child is currently living. In this meeting, the process is described as follows:"I need to meet with you today to find out your perception of what is going on between your child and the other parent. After I meet with you, I'm going to meet with the other parent to obtain their perceptions. This is not a case of forcing the other parent on your child. It is a process of addressing problems in building a healthy and appropriate relationship between the child and both parents. This process is not trying to replace you as a parent. When I meet with the other parent, I will first ensure that they are willing to follow my process. After having individual sessions with each parent and the child, I am going to have a session involving the parent and the child together.

    "In the first session, the child is able to tell the other parent everything that he or she is upset about. I am not interested in what the truth is, because there is no way we can ever determine what the truth is. What is important is what the child believes the truth to be. Before we can start addressing issues, we need to have the child list all of the problems. In that first joint session, and all subsequent sessions, I am not going to allow the parent to disagree or argue with the child. If the parent tries to argue, I will first give the parent a warning and if this continues, I will end the session. On a practical note, I would like you to arrive a few minutes early for the appointment and we will set you and your child off in a side room. The other parent is instructed to not arrive early and will be taken directly into my office. I will then come and get the child for the session.

"Your child will know that if they become uncomfortable and I have not noticed what has happened, they are able to ask to excuse themselves to use the bathroom and the child can then go back to the room you are in. If the child does not return in a few minutes, I will leave the other parent in my office and come to the room you are in to find out what is going on for the child. After all of the issues are listed, we will then go through them one by one, not to prove or disprove them, but to come up with a plan for how such things could not possibly happen in the future. There may be a point where I need to have a session with you and the child to get your help in encouraging the child to give the other parent a chance.

"As time goes by, if progress is being made, we want to slowly increase the contact between the other parent and your child. Typically how we do this is for the other parent to pick the child up from school, attend a session, and then you will be here to take the child home. If that goes well, the parent will then pick the child up, go for lunch, attend the session, and then the child will go home with you after the session. The time with the other parent and child is gradually increased and it always ends with a counselling session, even to have a morning session after the first overnight and a Monday morning session after the first weekend. This way, if anything did not go well, it'll first be observed by the therapist, so you will not be accused of alienation. Alternately, if things go well but later complaints are made about the session, it does identify if potential coaching activities are taking place that hamper the process."

2. Meeting with the Rejected Parent

The same description of the process and history taking is done with the rejected parent, as with the preferred parent. The need to listen and accept what is said by the child as the child's "truth" is emphasized, as is the need to work forwards without vilifying the other parent. A strict warning that appropriate behaviour must be shown is given and the therapist needs to make a judgment whether the parent appears to be willing to cooperate with the therapist's process or not. I emphasize that this is an open process and that any misbehaviour on the part of either parent will clearly be communicated to the court. As the parent relates the history, the therapist can intervene with coaching points and suggestions of how things could be done differently.

The parent is also told that for the first session they are not to bring gifts, pictures, the child's possessions or anything else, and that they can only do so in subsequent sessions with the therapist's permission. It is emphasized that they must not arrive early or even be outside of the building ahead of time, to prevent confrontations or misunderstandings. The parent is told that the child and the other parent will be leaving the office first, again to avoid unpleasant encounters.

3. Meetings with the Child

As was done with the parents, the entire process is clearly described to the child emphasizing their safety and that they are not going to be confronted by the rejected parent. Questions similar to those described previously for working with the individual child can be used to guide the child through a thorough description of the current situation and past difficulties. I usually tell the child that they will be able to decide if they want to meet with me once or twice to gain comfort before meeting with the rejected parent, but the child does not get the choice whether to meet or not. It is important to develop an itemized list of what the concerns are, while also looking forward to what positives could take place.

4. Parent-Child Meetings

In the first meeting, the parent is coached to listen, not disagree (which can include nonverbal headshaking, eye rolling or grunting), compliment the child on being brave, promise the child that he or she is not in trouble and now that the parent knows what is bothering the child, they can start working on solutions. If all that can be accomplished in the first session is developing the list (either by the child alone or with the therapist's help) and having the parent compliment the child for his or her honesty, it should be viewed as a successful session. It is better to have a shorter, positive session, than to have a longer session that becomes negative.

The parent is not asked to admit to things they do not believe happened, although if the parent did make mistakes, a sincere apology can go a long way towards healing. This is especially true if the parent has been verbally or otherwise inappropriate with the child. The parent can let the child know it was not the child's fault and that the parent takes the blame and promises such a thing will never happen again. If you are working in a therapeutic team, it can also be beneficial to take breaks where the therapist working with the parent can take them out of the room to offer coaching advice, while the child's therapist can also offer pointers for how the child can communicate more effectively.

The therapist picks the order of topics to address and helps the parent and child work through each issue, as to how things could be different in the future so that those issues will not re-emerge. As each issue is completed, the agreement is noted, although copies are not given to the parties. Once improvement is being seen, the time between the parent and child outside of the office is increased, as previously described, or other times are scheduled, such as going to a movie, attending events or watching the child in extracurricular activities. It may be beneficial at some point to have the parent bring in photographs of fun activities the two of them did together in the past.

One sign of the alienated child is that even after all the issues have been addressed, the child is still maintaining that he does not want to see the parent outside of (or even in) the office. At this point, a further individual session may be required with the child to find out if there are other reasons that have not yet been raised. Alternatively, having a session with the preferred parent and the child, in which the preferred parent tells the child, "I expect you to spend time with the other parent" can be helpful.

As an example, when working with a preteen, the relationship between parent and child appeared strong during counselling sessions, but there was a consistent refusal to even drive to the session with that parent. An individual session with the child uncovered the child's belief that the preferred parent would be upset if progress was made. This belief was communicated to the preferred parent and a session was held specifically to tell the child, "I am your parent and I am perfectly capable of looking after myself. I do not need you to do it for me and

I expect you to spend time with the other parent."
The following session the child asked if they could go
watch a movie together. An interesting point is even if the
preferred parent is an "alienating" parent, he or she will
verbalize the desire for the child to see the other parent
but then plead helplessness that they cannot force the
child. By setting up a situation where the favoured parent
has to direct the child to see the other parent, a double
bind is created. Even children are aware of the concepts
of honest and dishonest, and if the preferred parent says
one thing in therapy and another later, that parent can be
viewed by the child as dishonest.

Even children are aware of the concepts of honest and dishonest...

Experience and clinical judgment are always important in
any part of Family Restructuring Therapy and especially
in working with reunification. At times I have been pleasantly
surprised. We had a family with three children who were all
rejecting one parent. We carefully set up the process using two
therapists and reached the point of the initial (separate) sessions
between the rejected parent and the children. Each child listed
his or her concerns. The rejected parent demonstrated appropriate listening skills and reassured the children that they were not
in trouble. Then, each child spontaneously asked, "So can
I come over this weekend?"   Unfortunately, at the other end of
the continuum are the tragic cases where there would be a real
risk of harm to the child, either by their own doing or even by
the preferred parent, if forced into an increased relationship with
the rejected parent. Children, or parents, can threaten or play
the ultimate trump card of suicide in extreme cases. Such actions

require quick and decisive action by police or child protection authorities.

There is a very real reason why many of the families we work with in Family Restructuring Therapy have been labelled high-conflict and have had multiple appearances before the courts. When we are able to guide such a family into healthy behaviour it is indeed a positive event.

CHAPTER 10

Conclusion

In writing this book, it was my goal to share with the reader the philosophy of working with high-conflict separated and divorced families that has evolved in our partnership over many years. The title of the process, Family Restructuring Therapy, is purposeful. We are looking at the family through the eyes of the children. Parents can divorce and live in different homes and, unfortunately, even in different countries—but this does not end the concept of family for the child.

> This process helps families transition from dysfunction to function if the parents allow it to take place.

A key factor in Family Restructuring Therapy is that it is directive and requires highly skilled, experienced, ethical mental health practitioners who are not afraid to teach and lead in conducting therapy. This process helps families transition from dysfunction to function if the parents allow it to take place. There are excellent resources for the practitioner working with such families including: the *Family Court Review* and the *Journal of Child Custody*; the Association of Family and Conciliation Courts (AFCC), which should be viewed as an essential organization to be in for individuals wanting to work in this area; and obviously the work of Bill Eddy and the High Conflict Institute also provides excellent guidance.

Family Restructuring Therapy follows a systemic framework within the overall philosophy of humanistic psychology—with the belief that even dysfunctional parents are trying to do their best. If they can learn a better way to parent their children, there is a chance for behavioural change.

A tiny sample of some of the excellent research being done pertaining to parenting and divorce was provided in the sections on Shared Parenting and Bonding, more as a teaser to encourage the reader to explore this area more thoroughly, than to attempt to summarize the plentiful research in these areas. However, the one lesson from research, which appears over and over, is that conflict damages children. I am tired of working with children who draw family portraits with them in the middle with arms stretched out towards each parent like some kind of superhero made out of elastic. It is distressing to see 8-year-old children trying to meet the needs of their parents at the loss of their own childhood and well-being. Equally distressing are the mental health and legal professionals who think that a 12-year-old has the ability to make decisions with life-changing repercussions, even though they are not able to drive a car until 4 years later.

Within each area of law, psychology, social work or mediation there are many subsets. Working with custody issues is a completely distinct culture from family counselling or even traditional forensic psychology. It is essential that the mental health practitioner be educated in the laws, ethics, guidelines and culture of custody in order to be effective and in order to not cause harm.

Family Restructuring Therapy is demanding for the therapist. If you do not have the luxury of working in a group practice, then there is a need to affiliate with other like-minded professionals in your community for both personal support and to be able to break complex cases down by using a therapeutic team.

It can be highly satisfying when you are able to see a child relieved of the burden of having to choose sides or a set of parents learning how to communicate effectively, possibly for the first time. It can be frustrating when parents choose to continue the conflict, spend family resources on legal battles or require a judge to become the de facto parent for their children and to have the children live separate lives in parallel parenting arrangements.

I have tried to provide many practical interventions that can be used with high-conflict families, as I find it more successful to blame the processes, and to offer different processes, than to blame the individual parents. I would be very interested in hearing how others utilize and modify the concept of Family Restructuring Therapy in working with both "normal" and high-conflict divorce families.

Parenting Plan: List of Topics

The following pages contain a checklist of the topics parents may want to include in a parenting plan.

Some of the topics listed may be irrelevant to your family. Other topics may need to be broken down into many sub-topics. For example, some families are able to skip over the topic of allergies, while other families need to break discipline down into many parts (hitting, telling lies, refusing to do homework, skipping school, etc.)

Probably the most important factor pertaining to the upbringing of your children is the parents getting along and acting as a team. Keep in mind, no one parent "is the boss" and that there is a difference between your wishes and the final decisions made.

This booklet serves as a record for the dates which agreements were reached on various topics; it does not contain enough space to document the actual agreements. The agreements are typically documented, one issue at a time, on separate sheets.

Date
agreed

1   Schedule

    a.   Regular – majority of the year / school year

    b.   Summer holidays

    c.   Winter break

    d.   Spring break

    e.   How to modify/re-evaluate parenting plan

    f.   Relocation

2   Exceptions to the schedule

    a.   Extracurricular activities

    b.   Child/Family Birthdays

    c.   Mother's/Father's Day

    d.   Long Weekends

    e.   School holidays

    f.   How to request a change/trade

    g.   Travel request and information sharing

    h.   Special events

    i.   Making appointments (doctor, etc.)

3   Exchanges (drop-off/pick up)

    a.   How to do

    b.   Expected behaviour

4   Communication

    a.   Face-to-face

b. Telephone

c. E-mail / written

d Shared calendar

e. With child(ren) by parent

f. With parent by child(ren)

g With child(ren) by other (e.g. grandparent)

h About financial issues

i. Dispute resolution process

j. About changes in life / new partner, etc.

k Assistance with communication (counselling)

5. Parenting Issues

After/Before school care

Allergies

Allowance

Babysitters for the child(ren)

Babysitting (being allowed to)

Bedrooms (contents, sharing, etc.)

Bed-time

Birth control

Birthday parties (friends, extended family)

Breast feeding

Car seats

Cell phone

Chores

Clothing

Computer

Counselling

Curfew

Dating

Day care

Dental care

Discipline

Drinking alcohol

Driving lessons and restrictions

Drugs

Extracurricular Activity Selection

Extracurricular Attendance, Parent Involvement

Friends (parties, play dates)

Gifts for parents (birthday, other occasions)

Grandparent involvement

Guns

Hair style and colour

Health concerns

Home alone (after school, evening, etc.)

Homework

Hygiene

Illness – child

Illness – parent

Immunization

Internet

Lunches (school)

Nutrition

Knowledge of divorce

Movies allowed (ratings)

Music allowed

Name used

Parent-teacher interviews

Part time work

Passport

Pets

Physical fitness

Physician

Piercings

Post-secondary education

Prayer

Privacy

Reading

Religion

School events

School newsletters/communication

School pictures

School selection

School supplies

School transportation

Sexuality

Sex education

Siblings

Sleep over's

Sleeping with parent

Smoking

Step parent (name, involvement)

Tattoos'

Toilet training

Tutoring

Video games

Other:

Other:

Other:

Other:

Other:

Other:

Other:

Other:

References

Benjamin, M. & Irving, H. H. (1989). Shared Parenting: Critical Review of the Research Literature. *Family and Conciliation Courts Review*, 27 (2), 21-35.

Bowlby, J. (1969). *Attachment and loss: volume 1. Attachment.* London: Hogarth.

Bowlby, J. (1980). *Attachment and loss: volume 1. Loss.* New York: Basic Books.

Braver, S. L., Griffin, W. Eight. & Cookston, J. T. (2005). Prevention programs for divorced nonresident fathers. *Family and Conciliation Courts Review*, volume 43, number 1, January 2005. 81-96.

Brownstone, H. (2009). *Tug of war.* Toronto, Canada: ECW Press.

Dacey, J., Kenny, M. & Margolis, D. (2000). *Adolescent Development – Third Edition.* Carrollton, Texas: Alliance Press.

Eddy, Bill. (2008). *High Conflict People in Legal Disputes.* Scottsdale, AZ: HCI Press.

Elkind, D. (2001). *The hurried child: All grown up and nowhere to go.* Boulder, Colorado: Perseus.

Fidler, B.J, & Bala, N. (2010). Children resisting postseparation contact with a parent: concepts, controversies and conundrums. *Family Court Review*, 48(1), 10 – 47.

Finley, G.E. & Schwartz, S. J. (2010). The divided world of the child: divorce and long-term psychosocial adjustment. *Family Court Review*, 48(3), 516 – 527.

Fleming, D. S. (2002). *Promoting Healthy Child Development: A Population Health Approach.* Unpublished Doctoral Dissertation: University of Alberta.

Garon, R. J., Donner, D. S. & Peacock, K. (2000). From infants to Adolescents: a developmental approach to parenting plans. *Family and Conciliation Courts Review*, 38 (2), 168-191.

Gould, J. W. (2006). *Conducting scientifically crafted child custody evaluations (2nd Edition).* Sarasota, Florida: Professional Resource Press.

Gould, J. W. & Martindale, D. A. (2007). *The Art and Science of Child Custody Evaluations.* New York: Guilford Press.

Greenstone, J. L. & Leviton, S. C. (2002). *Elements of crisis intervention: Crises and how to respond to them (2nd Edition).* Pacific Grove, CA: Brooks/Cole.

Hayes, S. W. (2010). More of a street cop than a detective: an analysis of the roles and functions of parenting coordinators in North Carolina. *Family Court Review*, 48(4), 698-709.

Hirczy de Mino, W. P. (1997). Coparenting arrangements in a jurisdiction with statutory guidelines. *Family and Conciliation Courts Review*, 35 (4), 443-469.

Holtzworth-Munroe, A., Applegate, A.G. & D'Onofrio, B. (2009). Family Dispute Resolution: Charting a course for the future. *Family Court Review*, 47 (3), 493-505.

Insabella, G. M., Williams, T., Pruett, M. K. (2003). Individual and co-parenting differences between divorcing and unmarried fathers. *Family Court Review*, 41 (3), 290-306.

Jaffe, M. L. (1998). *Adolescence*. New York: Wiley & Sons.

Jaffe, M. L., Ashbourne, D. & Mamo, A.A. (2010). Early identification and prevention of parent-child alienation: A framework for balancing risks and benefits of intervention. *Family Court Review*, 48 (1), 136-152.

Jaffe, M.L., Johnston, J.R., Crooks, C.V. & Bala, N. (2008). Custody disputes involving allegations of domestic violence: toward a differentiated approach to parenting plans. *Family Court Review*, 46 (3), 500-522.

Johnson, J. R. (1995). Research update: children's adjustment in sole custody compared to joint custody families and principles for custody decision-making. *Family and Conciliation Courts Review*, volume 33, number 4, October, 1995. 415-425.

Kelly, J. B. (1993). Current research on children's post divorce adjustment: no simple answers *Family and Conciliation Courts Review*, 31 (1), 29-49.

Kelly, J. B. & Lamb, M. E. (2000). Using child development research to make appropriate custody and access decisions for young children. *Family and Conciliation Courts Review*, 38 (3), 297-311.

Kelly, J. B. & Lamb, M. E. (2003). Developmental issues in relocation cases involving young children: when, whether and how? *Journal of Family Psychology*, 17, 193-205.

Lee, S.M., Kaufman, R.L. & George, C. (2009). Disorganized attachment in young children: Manifestations, etiology, and implications for child custody. *Journal of Child Custody*, 6: 62-90.

Ludolph, P.S. (2009). Answered and unanswered question in attachment theory with implications for children of divorce. *Journal of Child Custody*, 6: 8-24.

Maida, P. R. (1991). Child support guidelines: a conflict analysis. *Family and Conciliation Courts Review*, 29 (4), 429-447.

McIntosh, J.E., (2009). Legislating for shared parenting: Exploring some underlying assumptions. *Family Court Review*, 47 (3), 389-400.

Miller, M.K. (2011). How judges decide whether social parents have parental rights: a five-factor typology. *Family Court Review*, 49(1), 72 – 83.

Moulton, R. (2009). Who's your daddy?: The inherent unfairness of the marital presumption for children of unmarried parents. *Family Court Review*, 47(4), 698 – 714.

Nielsen, L. (1996). *Adolescence: A contemporary view (3rd Edition)*. Fort Worth: Harcourt, Brace & Company.

Palmer, A. (2003). Parents' relocation after divorce may affect children long-term. *American Psychological Association Monitor on Psychology,* 34(8), 2003.

Pearce, J. W., & Pezzot-Pearce, T. D. (1997). *Psychotherapy of abused and neglected children.* New York: Guilford press.

Pruett, M. K., Ebling, R. & Insabella, G. M. (2004). Critical aspects of parenting plans for young children *Family Court Review,* 42 (1), 39-59.

Ricci, I (1997) *Mom's House, Dad's House: Making two homes for your child.* New York: Simon & Schuster.

Pedro-Carroll, J., Nakhnikian, E. & Montes, G. (2001). Assisting children through transition: Helping parents protect their children from the toxic effects of ongoing conflict in the aftermath of divorce. *Family Court Review.* October 2001, 377-392.

Seligman, M. E. P. (1996). *The optimistic child.* New York: HarperCollins.

Steinberg, L. (2002). *Adolescence – 6th Edition.* Boston: McGraw Hill.

Taylor, A. (1989). Shared Parenting – is it working? Reflections by a court service mediator. *Family and Conciliation Courts Review,* 27 (2), 7-16.

Thomas, R. M. (1985). *Comparing theories of child development(2nd Edition.* Belmont, California: Wadsworth.

Thompson, D. A. R. (2004). Movin' on: parental relocation in Canada. *Family Court Review,* 42 (3), 398-410.

Trombetta, D. (1989). Shared Parenting – is it working? *Family and Conciliation Courts Review*, 27 (2), 17-20.

Warshak, R. A. (2000) Blanket restrictions: overnight contact between parents and young children. *Family and Conciliation Courts Review*, volume 38, number 4, 422-445.

Warshak, R. A. (2007) Punching the parenting time clock: The approximation rule, social science, and the baseball bat kids. *Family Court Review*, volume 45, number 4, 600-619.

Zahn, M. A. (2007). The causes of girls' delinquency and their program implications. *Family Court Review*, 45 (3), 456-465.

About the Author

DR. STEPHEN CARTER has worked as a Registered Psychologist since 1992 and has also worked with children as an instructor, teacher and counselor since 1974. He specializes in working with adolescents and children in the areas of counseling and assessment as well as assessments and interventions with separated and divorced families. Along with working in private practice, Dr. Carter is an Adjunct Assistant Professor in the Department of Educational Psychology at the University of Alberta. He was previously an Executive Director of the Psychologists' Association of Alberta for several years.

He presented Family Restructuring Therapy at the Association of Family & Conciliation Courts Regional Training Conference in Indianapolis, Indiana in October 2011.

Dr. Carter has worked with children, adults and adolescents for many years and assists individuals and their families in dealing with serious problems including abuse, anxiety and depression, behavioural disorders, self injurious behaviour, relationship problems and work stress. Dr. Carter has delivered many workshops, presentations and media interviews on topics such as assessment, grief and loss, effective workplaces, conflict resolution, behavioral disorders, family restructuring therapy, high conflict divorce, school violence, stress management, ethics, running a private practice and expert witness testimony.

Visit Dr. Carter's website at www.familyrestructuring.ca.

CPSIA information can be obtained
at www.ICGtesting.com
Printed in the USA
JSHW022129161222
35060JS00001B/2

9 781936 268399